SHORT CUTS

INTRODUCTIONS TO FILM STUDIES

OTHER TITLES IN THE SHORT CUTS SERIES

SCENARIO

THE CRAFT OF SCREENWRITING

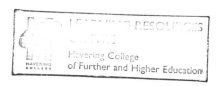
TUDOR GATES

WALLFLOWER

LONDON and NEW YORK

A Wallflower Paperback

First published in Great Britain in 2002 by Wallflower Press
5 Pond Street, Hampstead, London, NW3 2PN
www.wallflowerpress.co.uk

A catalogue record for this book is available from the British Library

ISBN 1 903364 26 4

Book Design by Rob Bowden Design

Printed in Great Britain by Antony Rowe Ltd, Chippenham, Wiltshire

CONTENTS

With grateful thanks to all my friends – especially Michael Zeffertt – for their advice and assistance in the preparation of this book; and to the late Lajos Egri, my guru.

INTRODUCTION

I first started my career, by a series of accidents, working backstage in the theatre. It exposed me to some wonderful plays, by Chekhov, Ibsen, Shakespeare, Shaw, Gogol, Dostoevsky, Sophocles and Sheridan, among others. I was also privileged to witness, night after night, some marvellous actors like Laurence Olivier, John Gielgud, Alec Guinness, Ralph Richardson, John Clements and Laurence Harvey – all of them splendid film actors as well.

It was a fine apprenticeship to the craft of writing, though I was unaware of it at the time. The plays I saw were timeless classics, some of which have been filmed many times (there were two filmed versions of *Hamlet* in the 1990s, three of *Romeo and Juliet*). I saw *King Lear, Julius Caesar, Henry V* and *The Taming of the Shrew*. I saw *The Cherry Orchard, Uncle Vanya*; *Pygmalion* and *Arms and the Man; Cyrano de Bergerac, Oedipus Rex* – and many more, all that I could possibly absorb at that time. It was an invaluable education.

Later I went on to become a stage manager, touring plays, most of them modern, most of them not very good. But one learns as much by bad example – what not to do – as by good example and, gradually, not consciously, I started to break down in my mind the components of these works. What was it that so clearly distinguished the banal from the classic? Why did some works hold their audiences in silent thrall, while others regularly induced prolonged bouts of coughing?

What was the magic recipe that in some cases created waves of laughter and applause, breaking endlessly across the footlights – as opposed to the polite but frigid reception accorded others? Was there an alchemist's formula? Could lead be turned into gold? I set off on the path of discovery. Was there some secret of writing plays, stories, films, episodes for television? Was it all a matter of inspiration or were there set rules that one could learn?

Was it possible that bad plays – for theatre, film or television – could be turned into good ones, that life could be breathed into the moribund? As a script doctor who has saved a few hopeless cases in my time, I believe it can. There is a set of principles which every writer should take to heart. Its formulation was not a revelation. I only found out what others had discovered before me. But I worked it out for myself, as you must arrive at your own conclusions – I can only guide you.

This book will help set you on a direct path. I learned the route the hard way, taking plenty of wrong turnings. When I embarked on a writing career, theatre was no longer mainstream entertainment, having been replaced by television. The big stories, with big casts, could now only be told on the big screen in the cinema – itself under threat from this poor but potent substitute. And the theatre play I had been trying to write, duly adapted, was eventually accepted as a film for television. The lesson learned here was that the principles of the craft apply to all forms of writing: it is only the techniques that differ. The ability to tell a good story is the key and Shakespeare would have been just as successful in Hollywood (he is) as he was in London, and paid a lot more.

This was the beginning of a career spent largely in working as a screenwriter, at first for television and then for feature films – interspersed with writing a few novels and then directing and producing. I did not return to the theatre for many years, when I was fortunate enough to have two plays produced in the West End, as well as many others that have toured the world. I have worked as a script editor for the BBC and as an advisor or doctor for both plays and feature films. After some years I arrived at a method of construction which will ensure a well-built literary edifice, that will survive even the roughest of criticism.

I truly believe that anyone can write well, if taught well. You need a command of the language, of course, and a belief in your own abilities. You need courage and determination as well as imagination. And you need to know those principles of construction so that you can critically analyse your own work and constantly strive to improve it. Re-writing is just as important as writing, perhaps more so.

I sometimes hold classes on this subject and I tell my students that I can help them construct a vehicle in the same way that I might show them how to build a car. If they pay attention and follow the instructions carefully, it will end up with four wheels and a gearbox and it will work: it will do what a car is built to do. It will go forward when you press the accelerator and it will stop if you put pressure on the brakes. However, I do not pretend to be able to tell you how to build a Ferrari or an Aston Martin. These are works of art which need more than a builder: they need a creator, the input of a spirit, a personality. All I can do is to show you how to build a car that works – the rest is up to you.

The background history that follows is by no means comprehensive: that would take a score of volumes like this. It is selective, an attempt to show how film was shaped over the course of the last century and how the skills of scenario writing were honed.

SO YOU WANT TO BE A WRITER?

You want to be a writer? I'm not surprised. I have been a professional writer throughout most of my life and I can tell you it is a job that has a lot going for it. I have been there and got the t-shirt, as a writer of abysmal clichés would say. I have mixed socially with the famous, had the chauffeur-driven car waiting for me at the airport, the first nights and all that. It can be a great experience but the job has its problems as well.

George Orwell claimed that writing was a horrible exhausting experience, like a long and painful illness. It *is* demanding. William Faulkner said that if a writer had to rob his mother, he ought not hesitate. George Bernard Shaw said: 'A true artist will let his wife starve, his children go barefoot, sooner than work at anything but his art.' I urge neither of these courses on you. Times have changed. Writers no longer live in garrets. These are more likely to be penthouses, carrying ruinous mortgage charges. To pay the bills you need concentration, lots of it. So you have to ask yourself *why* you want to be a writer. Is it to get rich? To mix with the stars? To be at the Oscars ceremony? None of these hopes is going to be the engine of success. Every fool dreams them. They may come, in due course, but they will only come from hard work, not wishing.

Writing is a lonely existence, initially anyway. It is all very different when eventually you get into production for a feature, a television film, or for the theatre. But that is a long way off if you are starting from scratch. Learning the craft of writing is no different from the study necessary to master any trade or profession. But remember, even when you have put in all the required study, you are still no more than an apprentice, and you still have to become a practising craftsman before you can go on to become a master. However, the end is achievable: writing is not an arcane mystery.

You may find the hard slog difficult. We are all of us impatient to succeed, especially when young, when we have a kind of arrogance, a conviction that we can do it quicker than others, take short-cuts that will go unnoticed. Obviously, people have different talents, different temperaments. You *may* be blessed with genius, in which case this book is probably not for you. I say probably because, if your genius goes unrecognised, you may well have to come back and take your place alongside the rest, learning the first principles.

We all hope to be lucky but you can't depend on luck. Chance does play a big part in all of our lives and you may be blessed by fortune, for a while. This is an industry where stars sometimes burn brightly but soon fizzle out. Hard work is the more dependable route to success: application, patience, determination – and a measure of talent.

The techniques which need to be applied to the various media are entirely different of course and so, by the way, is the manner in which the author is treated. I found that in the theatre the author was – and is – someone to be honoured. No one would ever think of changing a word of any play I wrote, without asking permission – and it was forbidden in the contract. Similarly, my experience in publishing is that although editors may make (often valuable) suggestions, no one changes the text without the author's consent. My recollections of a brief period spent writing for radio are similarly good. When you get into television, however, the writer by and large takes a back seat – and that is maybe what is wrong with a lot of television today.

Why this sudden change of status? The principal reason is that another creator has taken your place, stolen in like a cuckoo to hatch your issue. The person who will be responsible for the final shape of your piece on screen is the director. In fact the director is now recognised in legal terms as the author of a visual work, along with the producer. This does not affect your own copyright position as the author of the screenplay but now a distinction has been made between the script and the finished work, and you are just part of the collaborative process. Total control has been ceded to the director who will be the prime creator from now on – and you had better get used to that idea or you will go through agonies of artistic frustration. So either choose another medium or get on with it – or become a director yourself!

If you are a professional writer, if you have a family to look after, a mortgage weighing you down, various credit cards to pay off, it is usually not such a difficult decision. You swallow your frustrations as you would in a whole variety of job situations outside the world of entertainment, and you do your utmost – by cajoling rather than complaining – to get the best possible version of your script up there on the screen.

If and when you move into the world of feature films, you will probably think you have made it, but not so. You earn a lot more money but get treated a lot worse and I do not mean from any lack of hospitality, luxury hotels or limousines at your disposal. These are just the accoutrements of big picture-making but when you enter this new world you will find that there are many, many creative talents employed in constructing a movie and most of them want to express what *they* want, rather than whatever it is that you want. Fight it if you can but remember that only the bravest, or the most cunning, or the most philosophical, survive in this particular jungle.

Writers do fight back. In the United States, where union membership is obligatory for screenwriters, the Writers' Guild of America, after threatening strike action in 2001, has won from the producers – in addition to increased cash – a raft of new rights to buttress their members' creative status. Residuals (payments for repeat showings), which are of enormous importance to writers, will be substantially increased. There will be an entitlement for them to re-acquire their unproduced screenplays (a long-running sore) and to be present at cast-readings and to visit sets. Agreements now include provisions for new markets like DVD (digital video disc) and video-on-demand. There are ongoing negotiations about Internet payments. Writers will have an enhanced presence in press kits.

You may think this is discursive but there is no point in learning how to write if your skills are never going to be exhibited. Nor if you are never going to be paid properly. If you write a book you can publish it yourself, even if you distribute only twenty copies to your friends and relatives. If you are a painter, you need only the canvas and materials to display your work. But if you are a film-maker then you are part of an industrial process that starts to count in millions. Everyone wants an audience but good writing alone will not earn one: you will need to learn how to play the market as well. Being able to sell your work (or get it sold) is a skill just as important as the writing. A modest script that becomes a film will give you more satisfaction than a brilliant one hidden in a drawer. Far better to have got a movie made, even if it bombed, than never to have even seen your name up on the silver screen.

The difference between success and failure may not just lie in the persuasive skills of a good agent. There are ways of writing a script which, if adopted, will make it seem clearly professional, and will help disguise a lack of experience. Do not be confused by the simplicity of the rules: it is vital that they are observed. Do not gloss over what seems blindingly obvious: you may think it so but it is not. Even good screenwriters make mistakes and that is why script doctors exist, to find broken rules as a surgeon finds broken blood vessels.

What is it that you want to say? This is the core of good writing, to feel passionate about some aspect of life and to be able to express that passion. If your reply to the question is that you have this great idea for a story which has lots of action scenes, car chases galore, aeroplane crashes, death, destruction and general mayhem, then read no further: you are not a writer. A *voyeur* perhaps, a teller of sick jokes, but not a writer.

I get lots of scripts sent to me. I try to read them all. If they followed what I believe to be the simple rules of writing, I *would* be able to read them all and it would be a simple task for me to comment on them. But they do not. They are mostly a mish-mash, pages of dialogue and visual directions, usually half-remembered fragments of once-seen films. There is no theme, there is no purpose to these scripts. I have to rack my brains to try and work out what they are all about. They are more like hasty, badly put-together scrap-books.

You cannot just throw together a bit of James Bond, a few snatches of Tarantino, a dollop of Stephen King, and then think you have created something wild and original. Originality – in the sense of the work emanating from you, rather than being extraordinarily new – stands out a mile. If being a writer means anything, it means having a voice. *Your* voice, not someone else's. That is what will distinguish your work, because it is different and it is individual. Writing, in a sense, must be about you: not you as a character, but because it is your point of view that will highlight the story and give it depth and texture.

You may want to write thrillers, cop shows, love stories, soaps, comedy or action adventure, futuristic science fiction or historical romances. It makes no difference what genres you select, or whether you intend to write across all of them, as I have. The rules of the game remain the same.

WHAT'S IT ALL ABOUT, ALFIE?

What is the premise of your story? What is it all about? Michael Caine's Alfie struggled with the mysteries of the universe. Our search is more straightforward but has the same goal of establishing what *it* – in this case, your screenplay – is all about.

Think of a matrix – not the movie but an environment in which a culture can be developed, like a womb for example, fostering a child from foetus to birth. You can see the comparison. The story emanates from the seed of an idea but that seed needs a culture in which to thrive. The seed has an aim, a purpose, a premise, which is to be brought to life. If the premise is right, if the genetic material is sound, a strong and healthy child will be born. Maybe struggling against the light, loudly complaining about this introduction to a hostile world. But then, no one said it would be easy.

First of all, you have to be writing about *something*. You smile. The advice sounds almost infantile. You are writing about Fred and Jenny and how they met and – stop right there! That is just *storyline*. You are relating the first of a series of actions which may or may not be significant. What your story is *about* is something that *must* be significant.

Imagine someone telling you a story, a simple catalogue of actions. Even if the actions are very dramatic, unless you can relate to them in some way, the story will fall dead flat. Have you ever been to the movies but then, when you came out, wondered what the picture had been all about? There were good action sequences, perhaps, and top-class performances. There was striking camera-work, neat editing, smart dialogue. These are all aspects of movie-making that can be savoured and appreciated but, unless you get that feeling of fulfilment, that you have witnessed a complete and rounded story, you will be left feeling dissatisfied.

A story, to be complete and rounded, needs to be about something. It is a tale that has a point to make; it is not just a vague commentary or the relation of a few episodes. It needs to be the framework of a holistic experience, one which incorporates the input of all the creative personnel involved, so that viewing the end product will indeed be a rich and satisfying experience. And of all those talents (though the director will say something else), the writer's is the most essential, the most meaningful.

It is possible to have films which are brilliantly directed but which go nowhere, when the director loses himself in the clouds of his own ego. It is possible to have in a film magnificent art direction and radiant acting, but these and other artistic contributions will never get the recognition they deserve unless the film proves to be a success (critical or box-office, or preferably both), and you cannot have a successful film without a first-rate script. The corollary of this, of course, is that with a bad script, whatever you spend, regardless of the big names involved, the film will die. Here are just a few disastrous examples:

THE GREATEST STORY EVER TOLD
HEAVEN'S GATE
BONFIRE OF THE VANITIES
WATERWORLD

We need not go back to the Greek amphitheatre or the Elizabethan playhouse: what interests us more is the chain of events leading to the multiplex.

Various names have been associated with the creation of cinema and its paternity is still squabbled about by different countries. The British claim Friese-Greene and the French the Lumière brothers. The Germans put forward the claims of Max and Emil Sklandowsky while the Americans add the invention to the long list of achievements in the scientific field attributed to Thomas Edison.

For our purposes, it does not matter – we will give it to the French. What interests us more is the evolving process of telling *stories* in moving pictures, as opposed to the extraordinary sensation (as it was then) of seeing objects in motion, horses galloping, trains hurtling towards you. And the French also had a pioneer in George Méliès, a conjurer who transferred his skills on to film, turning female wrestlers into men and having ghosts dance – the first SFX man, no less!

Even so, these were still just disjointed episodes, projected to impress; an experience, like seeing the bearded lady in the circus. What the screen was crying out for was someone who could merge all these splendid visuals into a compelling narrative – to tell a story – and probably the first man who did that was an American, Edwin Porter, in 1903 with his *Great Train Robbery*, a title which has a certain ring about it, does it not?

It is a simple tale of good and evil which, like all good stories, has a beginning, a middle and an end. There is a robbery, a chase, and the arrest of the criminals. Above all, there is a cogent premise – crime does not pay! This was theatre on a grand scale, apparently limitless in its scenic invention – and all for a nickel admission fee. If ever there was a business destined for growth, this was it.

Over the next couple of decades the industry burgeoned, although there was no real Hollywood dominance as yet. Films were also being made in Great Britain, France, Germany, Italy and Denmark – and Russia, of course. Indeed, if there was a creative motor, it was probably to be found in cultural Europe, whose actors, directors and writers were soon to be tempted to the New World, and for good and compelling reasons.

What America had was growing prosperity (fuelled by exports to the warring European nations), peace, and a domestic market catering to a huge immigrant population. Most of them could not speak English but they could all understand the movies and their nickels were already grossing up to hundreds of millions of dollars.

This was, in a sense, the high tide of movie-making. For the first time, an art form had emerged that knew no boundaries of language or culture. True, there were captions to help the action along but they were unnecessary – and the audience could supply a dialogue track from its own imagination, or just by lip-reading, while live piano music was there to underscore the drama or the comedy.

Already it was clear that what audiences wanted were stories about characters with whom they could identify – if only in their dreams – spelling out a simple lesson which in some way enriched their lives. These basic requirements have never changed, from the parables in the Bible to those in Greek mythology and drama, through Shakespeare to modern-day theatre, and you would do well to remember that. Mankind's essential chronicles may have all been related before but there are literally countless variations on these fundamental plots and audiences never seem to tire of hearing the great stories told and re-told, over and over again.

Hollywood (I will call it that although production was geographically widespread) understood that, realising that this was the medium for the entertainment of the masses – worldwide! Chaplin and Keaton went down as well in China or India, even in the poorest villages, as they did in London or New York. The early moguls – the Warner Brothers, Jesse Lasky, Sam Goldwyn and the others – knew the sweet smell of big bucks, or any other currency, when it was in the breeze.

It was left to Europe initially – and Russia – to explore the artistic boundaries of film in the immediate post-war period. *Expressionism* was spawned in Germany while Sergei Eisenstein was experimenting with montage and developing advanced techniques in editing, visible in *Strike* and *Battleship Potemkin*. The Americans were less concerned with art than with bums on seats: their principal efforts were in the field of technical expertise, leading eventually, in 1927, to the release of the first motion picture with sound, *The Jazz Singer*, a cataclysmic event which was to revolutionise the film production industry universally.

Let us take a look at a couple of films, picked more or less at random, which may be said to epitomise that great era of silent films. Note how they are laying down the foundations for the sound motion pictures that are to come, and how strongly they depend on *story*, the narration of events, and how the elements of basic screenwriting are already established.

Compare and contrast them with the efforts of the British industry, already lagging behind. Here is part of a review written in 1921: 'Two British films illustrate what great strides the British film industry has taken during the last few years. One was *The Right to Live*, a Grunger-Davidson production. And the other, *The Narrow Valley*, issued by Hepworth. Neither of them contains a good story but they both set out to create an atmosphere, and both have succeeded.' *Neither of them contains a good story!* You could say the commercial film-makers were slow in catching on!

THE GENERAL (1926)

Possibly the last of the great silent movies, starring the incomparable Buster Keaton who, sadly, was not able to adapt to the invention of the talkies. The story is simple, good against evil, about an ordinary man – a train driver – whose blood is stirred when villains abduct both his locomotive and his fiancée (Marian Mack) who happens to be on the train at the time of the hijacking.

This film set new standards for the *chase* movie, translated into a wild, fast-moving comedy with some great visual gags and terrific stunts – none of which compromise the integrity of the basic story. It is this integrity on which your screenplay needs to be founded. There is a clear premise, that courage born of love will allow one to overcome all obstacles. The protagonist must be the engine-driver himself, whose heroic actions will bear out the premise, while the antagonists are the union soldiers who hijacked *The General* (the name of the locomotive), and the ensuing perils of the chase, the dangerous obstacles which the hero must overcome. Note these three terms: *premise, protagonist* and *antagonist*. They are the essential building blocks of any screenplay. The three most important questions you will have to ask yourself are:

(1) What is the *premise* of my screenplay?

(2) Who is the *protagonist*, who will establish the truth of my premise?

(3) Who is the *antagonist*, or what are the forces of antagonism, that will constantly put barriers in the path of the hero?

Let us take a look at another great film of this period, like *The General*, beginning to lay down the elements of the scenario and its translation into film.

THE GOLD RUSH (1925)

The *premise* here is that cheerful optimism helps one to survive even the most dire misfortunes. Clearly the *protagonist* has to be Charlie Chaplin, the ever oppressed, ever discriminated against, common man, while the *elements of antagonism* are the forbidding Klondyke itself, with its unbearably harsh conditions, and the unscrupulous characters it draws at the time of the gold rush.

The premise is classic Chaplin – pretty well the same theme of all his movies, the little fellow surviving against all the odds – because of his inner faith. It is not religion, it is the indomitable human spirit. Chaplin shows in this film that there are riches to be found in love and friendship of far greater value than gold.

The comic invention of the great mime genius is prolific here, and the pathos played to perfection. There are moments of cinematic history: the dance of the bread-rolls; the savouring of the laces and nails from his boots; the decrepit shack teetering on the edge of the icy precipice. This must be, along with *City Lights* and *The General*, one of the masterpieces of silent film. But what is Chaplin's genius? How is he able to make audiences weep or rock in their seats with laughter? Why are his stories so *satisfying*?

Let us start to look more closely at the components present in a good construction.

MAKE YOUR ARGUMENT

Think of how a debate is constructed in the House of Commons, say, or at the Oxford Union. 'This House believes that...' is the way the motion is phrased. It states an opinion. Someone makes the case. Someone then expresses an opposing point of view. Shades of opinion are voiced by the various contributors to the debate. In the end, either the proposer has convinced them of his argument, or he has not. Either way, a conclusion has been reached and a clear motion, whether amended or not, then stands. It is a statement of belief.

Think of a criminal trial. The audience here is the jury, not the spectators present. While they will almost certainly have their own views about the matter before, during and after the case, the conclusion will be the jury's. Prosecuting Counsel (let us make her a woman this time) sets out the case against the accused and calls witnesses and technical experts, perhaps, to support her argument. Defending Counsel (also female) rejects the case made out against her client. She takes all the points put forward by the prosecutor, in particular those which she fears might influence the jury, and tries to demolish them, bringing in her own witnesses and experts to counter the evidence given. The judge sums up and then the jury, after due consideration, gives its verdict. We know how nail-biting an experience it can be, waiting for a decision. Court-rooms are the very stuff of drama. They are the licensed theatres of the eternal conflict of good versus evil. They expose the vulnerability of human beings, they explore the high passions which motivate so many crimes.

There has to be an argument to sustain our interest. A plea of guilty is a total cop-out, even though the circumstances surrounding the case may be sensational, for the only matter in doubt is the length of the sentence. We have been robbed of pronouncing our own verdict. We want to hear the case made, and contested. We want to hear argument, denunciation. We want the outcome never to be certain. We want to witness a *conflict* as this is the heart of drama. There is conflict in *King Lear*, between Lear and his daughters. There is conflict in *The Taming of the Shrew*, between Kate and Petruchio. There is conflict in *Romeo and Juliet*, between the Montagues and the Capulets.

But conflict is not just between characters: there is also the conflict of ideas. That is why you must know what you are writing about, the theme of your story, the crux of your argument – in short, the premise. Without a premise, you have nothing to build on. No matter how lavishly you decorate your construction, it will surely disintegrate without a premise. The argument must be made.

Let us go back to *Romeo and Juliet*, a wonderful play that has also been translated into opera, ballet, and many excellent films. You may have seen Zeffirelli's lush version or perhaps Baz Lurhmann's marvellous contemporary interpretation. I have seen *Romeo and Juliet* performed many times, sometimes well, sometimes badly, and it is extraordinary how this beautifully crafted play survives even the most bizarre recountings. Why? Because it has a strong premise. It has a universal theme. The proposition is that true love cannot be defeated and will live on, even after death.

This is the argument made by the author, but since this is not a debate and he wishes to make his point in the form of a story, he begins by defining true love, having Romeo first complaining about yet another dalliance gone wrong, and then meeting by chance with Juliet, an encounter that has the power of a heavenly visitation. Until this moment, he had not realised the true meaning of the word *love*.

Is this going to be a beautiful romance then? The answer is, not without considerable hassle. The families of both young lovers are deadly enemies. There is not a snowflake's chance in hell of them ever agreeing a marriage – and anyway, Juliet's parents already have plans for her betrothal.

Young people, carried away by their emotions, ready to defy their parents – it is a situation that recurs throughout history and is even painfully, often tragically, still apparent today. In many cases, the story stops right there – the parents have their way, the arranged marriage takes place. But that is another story, which in no way reflects our premise. So far as we are concerned, without continuous conflict there is no story, and true love has to conquer all the obstacles placed in its path. Indeed, that is another way in which we can express our premise: that true love survives all barriers, even the ultimate one of death.

It seems that the whole world is against the star-crossed lovers although we know they will yet find allies. This is important because without a balanced struggle, there is no true conflict. But it is the power of their love which will provide the triumphant, if tragic, conclusion of the play.

The Capulets place Juliet under house arrest, until she marries Count Paris. Her only friends are her childhood nurse and the Friar whom she met through Romeo. He advises her on how to avoid the planned marriage, by taking a sleeping draught which will make it appear she has died. She will soon emerge from her catatonic state however and, before the day of burial, be able to escape from her resting place and elope with Romeo.

Except no one told Romeo. When he arrives at her bedside, he believes she really is dead. Because he cannot face the prospect of life without her, he takes poison and kills himself. When Juliet wakes, she is distraught to find her lover dead. She takes the same poison, to be re-united with him in the afterlife. A curse has descended on both their noble houses.

One can see a studio head today murmuring: couldn't the ending be just a tad more upbeat? The answer is that no, it could not. If Romeo and Juliet had survived and married, that would have been just another romance – and that is not what Shakespeare wanted to write. His premise was not 'Stay on course and eventually you will both live happy ever after'. His premise was 'Great love survives even death' and he proves it triumphantly. It may not be one with which we agree but there is no doubting the case has been made. Audiences spanning five centuries have never doubted its validity and it is rare for the tragic deaths not to move them to tears.

So the foundation of your screenplay must be a strong premise and we will go on to analyse other stories, and show you how to bench-test your own ideas.

Summarizing so far, you must understand that writing can be a low-paid, lonely and frustrating profession, and often is. But if you have a passion to write, if you are brimming with ideas (not plot-lines, *ideas*) that will illuminate your story, tell us something, make us see the world (even a tiny aspect of it) in a different light, then you will likely prove to be a good apprentice and, with courage and determination, go on to master your chosen craft.

Do not confuse ideas with stories. It has been said that there are only a finite number of plots and this may well be true. Certainly, the old Hollywood chestnut of 'boy meets girl, boy loses girl, boy gets girl back' can be interpreted in a thousand different ways – like in *Romeo and Juliet*, for example!

Remember, before you start writing, to ask yourself 'What's it all about?' Make sure that your understanding of your subject is a clear-eyed one. If you do not have a firm grasp of it, you can depend on it that we never will. We know the plot, one way or the other. You are only writing a variation of something that has been done a hundred times before. But that was by other writers. This time it is you who is making the argument, telling the story. It is your point of view that is going to make this story, this time, work for us, as it has never done with the others. It is what you have to say through your characters, in your words, that makes it different. Every writer is an individual, and needs to be, or we could get robots to write screenplays quite easily (sometimes I think they do).

Whether it is a play or a film, a contribution to a soap-opera or an episode for a series about policemen, nurses, firefighters, veterinary surgeons or what-have-you, it is the way that you see life that will make this particular episode seem new and refreshing for us, whatever the storyline may be. In an on-going serial or series, that may well have been dictated to you by the script-editors anyway. It should make no difference – so long as it is your premise, your original thinking, your philosophy that powers whatever you write. There is always another way to tell the story.

SOUND ... AND ALL THAT JAZZ

I was at an international conference held in Cannes recently, immediately prior to the Festival. I often attend such meetings and, frankly, get bored by the fixed and predictable attitudes of the different nations. Most Europeans object strenuously to the USA's domination of the world market. All of them plead for their own particular languages and cultures to be protected, usually by way of substantial state – now European, as well – subventions.

The English are in a somewhat different situation from the other Europeans because it is their language – although not their films – which is at the heart of all this cultural unrest. In addition to which, it is the film studios of the United Kingdom, and their technicians, that have long operated as a service industry for the Americans.

Just take a glance at some (a very few) of these great so-called American pictures:

SAVING PRIVATE RYAN
GLADIATOR
SCHINDLER'S LIST
INDIANA JONES AND THE TEMPLE OF DOOM
STAR WARS
E.T.

ALIEN
2001: A SPACE ODYSSEY
FULL METAL JACKET
WHO FRAMED ROGER RABBIT
THE SHINING
STAR WARS: EPISODE VI – RETURN OF THE JEDI

None of them are really American, of course. They were all made in Britain, largely with British technicians and actors. They qualify as American pictures only because they were US financed. Why do British investors not source these same films? Good question. If they did, we would probably have a viable British film industry, which we do not have. You will find there are many other references to this throughout the book. It is important to you, as a would-be professional, to understand the politics of the industry, as well as its history. It is the world market in which you will operate.

It was the advent of sound which crucified the continental European industry: where once their films had shown worldwide, now they were limited to those audiences who could understand the dialogue. Some of the great silent films are still with us, and well worth seeing, but cinema audiences from then on clearly preferred to listen rather than to read the titles – remember, there were plenty who could not even read – and so a new ball game began. America was technically ahead of this game and English was the most widely understood language in the world. Countless immigrants watched these films not just as entertainment but as a learning experience. Many still do and not only immigrants. Why do you think the continental Europeans – and I am thinking of the Nordic peoples in particular – speak English so well, while the English-speaking nations in general have such a poor grasp of foreign languages? It is not just their excellent systems of education. They are brought up watching English dialogue films. If we had enjoyed a similar experience, watching foreign language films – and I don't mean the occasional trip to an art-house cinema – we would doubtless be more proficient ourselves.

The US had an enormous domestic market and was not slow to latch on to the possibilities of forging the necessary organisations for sales and distribution throughout the world – it already had a foothold. True, most of the cultural talent resided in Europe but America has never been shy of buying the best. Even during the Great Depression, the movies prospered. People desperately needed something to take their minds off their problems and movie-going was affordable, even for the poor. Once the Wall Street Crash had occurred and the dust had eventually settled, the markets were ready to take off again. Exporting opportunities were tremendous, while the same parties involved in the First World War (to which America was a late, late entry) shaped up for a second bout, albeit with a couple changing sides. The stage had been set for the great boom years of the late 1930s and early 1940s, when big-screen entertainment really arrived as a force, over which the American retained a firm grip.

Just think of the enormous technical advances made during the 1930s, a decade which started with sound still scratchy and in its infancy and ended with *Gone With the Wind*, with a splendid soundtrack which included great effects and inspiring music, with a host of international stars all shot in gorgeous state-of-the-art Technicolor. What a sensational move forward. What breathtaking ambition! A lengthy best-seller about the Civil War had been translated onto the screen, setting new standards for every single aspect of film-making. The first truly great block-buster had arrived.

Let us examine another couple of milestones in movie history.

ALL QUIET ON THE WESTERN FRONT (1930)

This was the first great anti-war film of the sound era. It showed that the studios need not be confined to turning out escapist entertainment; they could produce serious, thought-provoking material as well. The premise is that there are no victors in war, only victims. The protagonist is played by Lew Ayres, as a handsome young German soldier – this was remarkable on its own, a film shown from an enemy point of view

– who volunteers with his friends to serve at the front. They believe with great, if misguided, sincerity in their Fatherland and the justice of their cause – romantic conceptions which are soon forgotten in the mud-filled, blood-soaked trenches.

This was quite a courageous picture to make twelve years after the end of the Great War and served as a signpost towards the future of movie-making, not just because of the evocative use of sound but the innovative direction of Lewis Milestone, in particular the panoramic effects achieved by use of a giant crane. There are moments of genuine visual poetry within the film, including the final shot, of a soldier reaching out for life – represented by a fluttering butterfly – before being brutally cut down by a sniper's bullet.

The film is a bitter condemnation of the war-mongers, who are the antagonists, as are the sapping, mind-crushing, squalid conditions of the trenches. The screenplay was based upon a novel by Erich Maria Remarque, another pointer towards the way movies were going. Then as now, there was trust in the material provided by best-selling books. The story had already successfully proved its popularity and would doubtless draw millions of readers to see it as a film.

All Quiet on the Western Front remains a fine film, well worth seeing, and is deserving of the too often misused epithet 'classic'.

DUCK SOUP (1933)

It was the time of the Great Depression and people wanted to forget their miseries. The cinema offered them a place of refuge, a chance to escape. Their dreams were projected on to a silver screen: they could be swashbuckling adventurers like Douglas Fairbanks or Errol Flynn; romantic songbirds like Nelson Eddy and Jeannette McDonald; or they could revel in the antics of the Marx Brothers, whose humour derived from not just zany visuals but also smart gag-lines, destined to become the stuff of legend.

Ruritanian settings were also popular at that time – another way of escaping to never-never land – and *Duck Soup* affords the Marx

Brothers the chance of delivering a satire on war wrapped up in their own brand of surrealist humour (a clear line can be traced back from *Monty Python* to *The Goons* to Groucho, Chico and Harpo).

Groucho, as always, is the protagonist, wooing and winning the formidable Margaret Dumont with his usual asides and in-your-face insults. The story (though not the premise) is for once irrelevant – Groucho somehow becomes the President of Freedonia, which is at war with the adjacent state of Sylvania (shades of the Balkan conflicts). This film – bettered only perhaps by the later *Night at the Opera* – was one of the founders of American smart-talking comedy. The humour of insult was born and it was not long before every New York cab-driver was wise-cracking like an entertainer.

THE PLAY'S THE THING

There is an interesting little sub-plot in *Hamlet* where the Prince constructs, for a travelling group of players, a murder mystery – one which is intended to prick the conscience of his own step-father, whom he suspects of having murdered his father. It teaches us the power of drama – at any level, if it is relevant, if it touches our lives.

In drama, the premise does not stand alone. It serves as a useful thumb-nail sketch, one which we have to convert into a detailed screenplay of a hundred or so minutes duration. We will need *characters* to put forward our arguments, and *characters* to oppose them. A deep, underlying *conflict* is necessary to sustain interest throughout.

There should be in every premise an element of universal truth. You will find many useful premises in the Bible, usually expressed as parables – mini-dramas in themselves – or in the words of old proverbs which, however hackneyed they may be, have stood the test of time. It is because of their relevance, because of their longevity, that they have become hackneyed – by constant use!

'All that glitters is not gold' has a host of applications. It is the Dick Whittington story; it is *A Star is Born*; it is any tale which concerns the painful process of learning what the true values are in life. You can, from your own experience, probably think of several examples, where people you know have suffered bitter disappointments as a result of their own ignorance, or innocence. To make a story, they have of course to survive, they have to be able to turn whatever impediments they encounter as stepping stones to success. In short, they have to have learned something about life.

After a trip to the cinema, or the theatre, we want to feel that whatever film or play we have seen has been an experience, and that it has taught us something, whether serving as a warning or reaffirming our own beliefs. Proverbs, parables, wise sayings, oft-repeated quotations, are minimalist lessons. Look at how some of the great phrases in literature have stayed with us:

'The moving finger writes and, having writ, moves on.'
'Do not ask for whom the bell tolls, it tolls for thee.'
'To err is human, to forgive divine.'
'There is honour amongst thieves.'
'Oh, what tangled webs we weave, when first we practise to deceive.'
'Hell hath no fury like a woman scorned.'

I wonder how many films you remember using that last premise – other than *Fatal Attraction*? What about the parables you might have learned in bible class, of *The Good Samaritan* or *The Prodigal Son?* The mythical tales of *Orpheus* or *Hercules*?

If I were teaching a class of a dozen people, and set them the task of translating any one of these into stories, I would expect very little, if any, duplication. That is because story-telling depends heavily on personal knowledge and all of us, through the make-up of our genes, through our schooling, our domestic environment, our experiences in love and war, are individuals.

ranks high in any list of post-war writers. The screenplay from his novel is credited to another major novelist, who also carved a career in films, William Faulkner.

This is *film noir par excellence*: mean, moody, sultry and sexy – and that is just Lauren Bacall. The chemistry between her and Bogart is extraordinary. No wonder they went on to become a real-life and long-running love story. Howard Hawks directs this incredibly complex plot with verve – re-makes have never challenged the original.

It is General Sternwood, who kicks the story off, hiring Marlowe to keep his nymphomaniac daughter out of trouble – a more than promising start. But nothing fazes Marlowe. He just loves putting spoiled society bitches in their place, and the dark, antagonistic world of blackmailers, pornographers, drug addicts and hired killers is familiar territory. Marlowe himself is the protagonist, once he decides that he is being used as a patsy, wearily ploughing through the field of mud they lead him into, wisecracking his way to the truth, even if it hurts. Philip Marlowe, although he would never admit it, is a man of honour and beneath the fedora and belted raincoat there is concealed a knight in shining armour. Although he claims he hates the job and only does it for the money, we know there is a lot more to it than that. When Marlowe makes a deal, he carries the job through to the bitter end – literally.

If *The Maltese Falcon* established the *film noir* genre, *The Big Sleep* confirmed its durability. Witty, incisive dialogue illuminates a labyrinthine story played out by instantly fascinating, well-drawn characters that, although moving maybe in a different social circle from us, and certainly from Marlowe, are still entirely believable. If you haven't already seen it, take a look, and learn. If you have seen it, take another look. Make an analysis of the plot, so far as you can.

BICYCLE THIEVES (1948)

This film was like a whiplash. For years the Italian people had been fed Fascist state-sponsored glamour movies, but life was not like that. Real life was picking up the pieces after the war, repairing the devastation inflicted by both the Germans and the allies, struggling to find employment.

One such victim finally lands a job, only to be unable to carry it out because his bicycle has been stolen. The premise is that with courage and determination, you will always find a way out of despair. The bill-sticker hero, together with his small son, set out on a journey through the poorest quarters of the city to find the bicycle. Director Vittorio de Sica takes an unsentimental view of the poverty of the population: this was the new realism. He is harsh towards both the political establishment and the Church, who are the principal antagonists, a courageous standpoint in Catholic Italy.

The unemployed man *has* to get his bicycle back, or steal another: without it there will be no work for him, no future to offer his son. His quest takes on mythical status. His life depends on achieving his goal, on defeating those who would frustrate him. It is the classical role of the protagonist.

If this sounds like a grim and forbidding film, it is not. There is a warmth, a love of humanity, a gentle romanticism which lifts the film to another plane and makes it without doubt one of the most important films of the generation, a turning point in the history of the scenario. It was nominated for an Oscar in the category of Best Screenplay.

MACBETH AND *RESERVOIR DOGS* (1992)

Let us assume that you have now carefully mulled over the story you have in mind, have analysed it and found the irreducible core – the premise. Now that we know this story is going to be about something, we want to know who is going to tell us that, and why. Who is going to put forward the proposition, who will make the argument, which of your characters is the one whose personality, whose inner drive, will force the tale to its logical conclusion. Whoever that is will be the protagonist, without whom there is no conflict. Do not confuse the protagonist with being the hero/heroine, or the principal character. That may be the case, or it may not. *Macbeth* – also the fore-runner of many fine films – may be an eponymous tale, about the man himself, and it may be a wonderful role, but it is Lady Macbeth who instigates the action. The premise of the play is stated clearly within the text: it is that of 'vaulting ambition, which o'er-leaps itself'. But the Thane of Cawdor's aspirations pale beside those of Lady Macbeth. It is her ruthless ambition which drives Macbeth to murder, and it is she who is the protagonist of the piece.

An interesting example of the non-hero protagonist can be found in *Reservoir Dogs*, the low-budget movie with which Quentin Tarantino burst on to the scene. Its premise is that there is honour amongst thieves. Eight men plan a jewellery robbery. Joe Cabot is the mastermind and his son Eddie, the bagman. The other six will carry out the crime and their identities are known only to Joe. Each has been given a pseudonym: Mr Brown, Mr White, et cetera.

Who is the protagonist? It is Joe Cabot, whose meticulous planning sets up the heist. Joe cares for the safety of his accomplices and his way of protecting them is for none of them to know the other. That way, if it all goes wrong, no one will be able to give evidence against anyone else. Except perhaps against Joe and his son, Eddie. But Joe trusts them. There is honour amongst thieves.

Who is the antagonist? It is Mr Orange who, in fact, is an undercover cop. He is a man of honour too, faithful to his calling, pursuing a dangerous game. We never see the robbery, just its aftermath and, in flashback, part of the planning process. They get the jewels but it all goes wrong when Mr Blonde, a psychopath, starts shooting up the staff. The waiting police open fire and there is a bloody battle. Brown and Blue are killed but, one by one, the others make it back to their rendezvous. White, who has buddied up with the undercover cop, wants to get him to hospital. Orange is badly wounded, shot in the guts.

The psychopathic Blonde has captured a uniformed policeman as a shield if the cops turn up at the warehouse rendezvous. By now there is a strong suspicion that the gang were set up and Blonde tortures the cop to get information. There is a horrific scene where he cuts off the cop's ear.

Eddie Bagot arrives with the good news that their haul is worth more than $2 million – but what a price they paid for it! Blue and Brown are dead and Orange is dying. They go outside to get rid of two of the cars, leaving Blonde to watch over the hostage and the dying Orange. Blonde returns to his game of mutilation but is pumped full of holes by Orange – it is only now that the audience learns his true identity.

As was confirmed later, both with *Pulp Fiction* and *Jackie Brown*, Tarantino is brilliant at manipulating time. He edits past and present to achieve maximum effect. The climax of the picture is a magnificent Mexican stand-off, worthy of Sergio Leone.

The others return, shortly followed by Joe Cabot, the boss. Orange tries to explain Blonde's death away by saying that Blonde had been planning to shoot the others and escape with the loot, but neither Joe nor his son Eddie buy that. They knew Mr Blonde very well as a loose cannon but still a loyal and faithful colleague, who had served time rather than grass on Joe or Eddie. For that, they honour him.

Joe draws his gun on Orange – who has to be the guy who set them up. White draws on Joe and threatens him. Eddie in turn aims his gun at White. The only other gang-member left now, Mr Pink, pleads for them all to stop this and get away while they can.

Joe Cabot cannot let his authority be challenged. This man Orange was a traitor. He entrapped them. Joe fires at the undercover cop and White shoots Joe. Orange was his friend: he trusted him. Friends protect each other. Simultaneously, Eddie fires at Mr White, who shoots him back. Both men collapse. It is a scene of carnage. Mr Pink grabs the jewels and runs for it – but outside the police are waiting.

Both White and Orange are still alive. White cradles his buddy and consoles him. Prison may await them but they are still survivors. When the police burst in, Orange calls out to them that he is a cop. Now, for the first time, White knows for sure that the man he befriended really did set them up. Honour dictates that he shoots Orange between the eyes before being blasted away himself.

Reservoir Dogs was a remarkable directorial debut by someone who is a natural storyteller. If this had been a big-budget picture, which was sneak previewed, I do not doubt that the test audiences would have written on their response cards that they were disappointed at the last-minute death of the heroic undercover cop. And I do not doubt that most studio heads would have ordered a more sympathetic ending.

But this film was not about the hero – he was the antagonist of the story. It was about honour. Men joined in such a dangerous undertaking can never rat on each other. Thou shalt not grass, under pain of death. And so White, a man of some decency and compassion, whatever his criminal record, had to execute someone he had considered his friend. No one, but no one, offends against the code. That was the necessary act for Tarantino to prove his premise. The picture was about honour and respect, not happy endings.

The same comment can be made about *Se7en*. The ending was downbeat, to say the least. The hero's wife had been decapitated by a psychopathic killer who then presented him with her head in a hatbox. It was tragic but it was necessary. The last of the seven deadly sins had to be played out – *Wrath* – and it fell to the Brad Pitt character to prove the premise.

As director, Tarantino never loses sight of his *premise*. It is Joe Cabot, who sets up the crime in *Reservoir Dogs*; he is the *protagonist*, though never the hero. It is Orange, the undercover cop, who intends to thwart the robbery and so becomes the *antagonist*. The *conflict* between the criminal elements and the forces of law and order is there from the beginning, as is the tension which rises steadily from the beginning to the end. The *characters* are beautifully orchestrated: each one of them does what he has to do and we never doubt their authenticity: they are the products of their backgrounds.

It is always so easy to empathise with the hero or the central figure and then lose sight of the story because you have not accurately identified the protagonist. Another classic example is *Othello*; we may be magnetised by the majestic stature and brooding presence of the tragic Moor general, but it is Iago who is the dynamo of the play, driving the premise, whispering venom into his master's ear until the great man is consumed by his own jealousy and both he and Desdemona become the victims of that malevolent passion.

THE BRIDGE ON THE RIVER KWAI (1957)

We have arrived at the point of considering character now. It is through the characters of your film that you will gradually expose your premise and it is they who will prove it for you. The protagonist is obviously the key character.

If I were an actor with the ability to read and analyse scripts, and if I were able to choose my role, it would always be the protagonist rather than the central character, or lead role. *The Bridge on the River Kwai* was about two men's conflicting notions of honour and it was the Alec Guinness character who was the protagonist.

The obligatory role of the American hero, coming to blow up the bridge, was played by William Holden, a much bigger star than Guinness at the time, but it was the British actor who picked up the Oscar because this was more than just an action-adventure story. It was about a clash of cultures, it was about the inner forces that impel men to their destinies – and that is why it was a magnificent film.

Incidentally, the story of how *The Bridge on the River Kwai* came to be made illustrates very well the importance of the scenario. Producer Sam Spiegel had hawked his existing script around quite a lot and it had been turned down by several directors, among them John Ford and Howard Hawks, before David Lean entered the loop. Lean just shrugged off Spiegel's script: it was the source material that interested him, Pierre Boulle's stunningly successful novel.

Another point that ought to be made is that the rejected script – by the eminent Carl Foreman – could hardly have been bad: it was not what Lean wanted and he did not believe it was faithful to the book.

the ending was a total cop-out, resolving nothing, which may explain why the film was not so successful in the UK. Certainly, it was well-made, had good performances and excellent production values, but it achieved a solution pandering to sentiment and populist culture, and not based on logic – which is why it was not a good film, and not well-written.

What rules of engagement are there for constructing a well-made script?

THE GRAMMAR OF WRITING

What makes a film innately satisfying is that a set of logical principles have been recognised. All premises entail conclusions. We infer that which is implied in the premise. The study of logic includes 'laws of thought' and if these are denied, then – whether you are aware of their existence or not – you will feel an unease, a dissatisfaction, because your premise has not been proved, or because an antithetical premise has been introduced. Your premise can be opposed: indeed, it must be in order to provide the conflict required, but to try to tell a story involving different and contradictory premises is both silly and muddle-headed – yet common enough.

You could think of these rules, if you like, as a grammar of writing. A sentence does not exist if it does not have a subject and a predicate. Something leads to something else. The verb expresses the action. Think back to some of the premises we have established: 'vain ambition leads to destruction'; 'great love survives even death'; and you will see the basic, logical, grammatical form your writing must take.

Take a very simple sentence: John loves Jill. It has a subject, who is John; an object, Jill; and a predicate which describes the relationship between the two. Every sentence must have a verb and verbs denote action. There is an activity, which is the act of loving.

It is a positive action. If the sentence had read 'John hates Jill', it would have been a negative action and an immediate precursor of conflict. But 'John loves Jill', in extension, can also lead to conflict. What if the sentence instead had read 'Romeo loves Juliet'? Because we know that the Montagues and Capulets, the families of the star-crossed lovers, are bitter enemies, the simple statement that Romeo loves Juliet (or that John loves Jill, in similar circumstances) takes on a whole new meaning.

It is a series of actions which will lead to a premise, the illustration of which will be your screenplay. There is probably not a lot to say about 'John loves Jill', standing alone, but if you expand it to include 'but Jill is married to someone else', you have created a scenario in which the drama is inherent.

David Lean once said that *Doctor Zhivago* was 'about a man who is in love with one woman but married to another'. There you have it. We remember the train scene, the winter palace, the charge of the Cossacks; we recall the epic scale of the historical background, the First World War, the Russian revolution. But what the film was about was one man's struggle with his own emotions. A largely autobiographical novel by Boris Pasternak, published (though not in Russia) in 1957, winner of the Nobel Prize for Literature the following year, it was the essential *truth* of the story which appealed to the director; its humanity and its passion.

The screenplay for *Doctor Zhivago* was written by Robert Bolt. I knew Robert and he told me of the immense difficulties he had in translating the book to the screen, a task which meant reducing the total content to about one twentieth of the original. In a sense this was good because it meant – although it took countless hours of heart-searching and many battles with David Lean – that he had to excavate the very core of the novel, its thrust and central purpose.

This is the task that awaits you, whatever the material you work with, and I urge you, before you write anything, to make that search, to formulate your premise as an essential first step. If you have already written a screenplay, then take another look at it. Study it carefully and break it down, not just into numbered scenes, or as a shooting schedule:

instead, dissect it analytically. Where is the heart? What is it all about? Forget the detail of the story, just try to grasp the sense of it. Can you reduce that to a single sentence? Is there a subject and a predicate? Can your statement be seen as a premise? Does it contain that element of universal truth? Are you writing about something in which you passionately believe?

Yes? Good. Let us learn a little more about the different genres of film, in which you might want to write. Do not try to run before you can walk.

ON THE BOX

The late 1940s were fascinating years in movie history. Although it was on a small screen, and in black and white, at last you could see films from the comfort of your own living room. It was inferior entertainment but it cost nothing, not directly anyway. The moguls responded as they always do. Make 'em big. Make 'em in colour. Spend, spend, spend. For a while, we had such technical innovations as Cinerama, the 70mm screen, and films shot in 3-D, which I personally found delightful – pity about the cardboard spectacles one had to wear to see them.

These desperate remedies worked for a while but the encroachment of television was remorseless. The mass audience which cinema had created was now fragmented and glued to the box instead. In truth, the world would never be the same again – not for movies, shown in cinemas – though it is interesting that the public's passion for watching films has never waned. It is just the delivery systems that change, as they are now, even as you are reading these words. But, and this is our predominant interest, how did the *content* of the films change? What were the new influences affecting writers and directors. How much would a resurgent industry in post-war Europe make itself felt?

The Italians were making films like Rosselini's *Rome, Open City,* developing a neo-realistic school probably started by Luchino Visconti.

The Bicycle Thief was a universal success, receiving an Oscar nomination for best screenplay and winning the foreign language award.

By the time of the 1950s, it was the French who were breaking new ground, establishing the right of the director to be known as *auteur. La nouvelle vague* turned critics into movie directors – well, *auteurs,* as they would have it. The phenomenon of the *film noir* was recognised.

There were fine films made in Japan at this time, when Kurosawa was establishing himself as a new creative source. Sweden gave us the enigmatic studies of Ingmar Bergman.

What was happening concurrently in Britain? Not a lot, although the series of splendid Ealing comedies have stood the test of time. It was during the 1960s that the Americans colonised Europe. It was cheaper to make films over here and, since they were spending big bucks and every buck counted, they wanted their money's worth up there, on the screen.

A MEMOIR

I wrote my first film, called *Troubled Waters*, for Sagittarius in 1962. It starred Tab Hunter. In 1966, I wrote a film for Rank called *Dateline Diamonds*. Both were inexpensive thrillers. I had already been working in television for a while and had devised and script-edited a series of my own for BBC, titled *Vendetta* (shades of *The Godfather,* yet to come). In 1967 I was invited to Rome to write the script of a Mario Bava horror movie and we then went on to make *Danger Diabolik* for Dino Di Laurentiis, a thriller comedy based on a cartoon series featuring, among others, the late Terry-Thomas.

I wrote a film, *Better a Widow,* starring Virna Lisi, for another Italian producer and was then engaged by Di Laurentiis to write the final draft of *Barbarella*, a big-budget sci-fi movie, also based on a cartoon series, starring Jane Fonda and directed by her husband Roger Vadim.

It was a difficult assignment, especially having to re-shape the words of an Oscar winner (indeed the words of several distinguished writers who had been previously employed on the script) but the end result was a big success. Jean-Claude Foret's brilliant imagination (it was his cartoon series) made it something of a cult movie and so it remains to this day.

Also working in the Di Laurentiis Studios at the time were Marlon Brando and Elizabeth Taylor, on *Reflections in a Golden Eye*, while *Waterloo* was being prepared down the corridor from my office. Eddie Dmytryk was shooting *Anzio* on location a few miles away while in Rome Clint Eastwood was busy with his spaghetti westerns. I was also lucky enough to meet Sergio Leone who, as well as directing all those fabulous Eastwood films, went on to write what I believe is a genuine cinematic classic, *Once Upon a Time in America*.

They were golden days which, like all things good, had to come to an end. In 1969, the US tax authorities changed their fiscal rules. It was no longer beneficial to the Americans to make their films overseas and those resident in Europe repatriated with haste. It was the end of an era.

Before that, however, the American industry's prosperity had rubbed off onto our own film-making activities. A new and temporarily confident breed of entrepreneurs gave us some fine films and allowed the great talent of British acting to flourish. Among others, Albert Finney emerged as a star after *Saturday Night and Sunday Morning*, and *The Adventures of Tom Jones*, which won four Oscars. Michael Caine was discovered in *Zulu*. We made *Oliver* and *Darling*, *The Ipcress File* and the James Bond films, bringing a young actor called Sean Connery into the public eye.

I worked for Harry Salzman once, the producer of the James Bond films. He told me that at the first public preview of *Dr No* in 1962, he and Cubby Broccoli were waiting nervously in the foyer for the audience's reaction. When they heard laughter, they were horrified: this had been intended as a tough, action picture, not a comedy. In fact, Terence Young's tongue-in-cheek direction gave the Bond films their style and verve, establishing a formula which has changed little over the years, although it has developed – almost into an art form. Kitsch art perhaps, but still immensely enjoyable. All that is really different about them is the size of the budget, the latest version rumoured to be topping $100 million.

You too can write a $100 million picture. Read on.

STARTING TO WRITE

Let us go back to the beginning again. Except that by now, I hope, you do not just want to write, you know what you want to write about. You have a premise for your story, you have a statement to make, and it is something you feel passionate about. I am wary about using phrases like 'you have a statement to make', which can sound pretentious, and often is. I well remember being at a production meeting for my first West End play, to discuss the set. There was a very nice model on show and the designer was taking us through its various aspects. When we got to the floor, to which I admit I had never given much thought, the director said profoundly: 'I do think the floor should always make a statement, don't you?' The others muttered a general assent. I could not think of anything pertinent in reply since my only concerns about the floor area were that it should be big enough to accommodate the action, and reasonably level. My barbarous thoughts may have been on a level with those of Sam Goldwyn when he said 'If you've got a message, send it by Western Union', but he was wrong, concerning writers. I am clearly no expert on floors but I have done an awful lot of writing and, believe me, unless there is something you have to say, there will be no content, no body in your work. It has to be about some aspect of life that deeply concerns you.

It makes no difference whether you are penning a horror flick or an episode of *The Bill* for television, or a ten-minute film for Channel Four, your story should say something. Take a look at *NYPD Blue* or even a light comedy like *Frasier* – there is no mystery about why they have consistently topped the ratings over so many years: they have interesting and insightful scripts. True, they have fine actors playing fascinating characters, and absorbing relationships, but there is more to it than that: each episode *says* something.

Let us suppose you want to write about the nature of friendship – what its limits are, or should be – and the nature of love – whether it has *any* limits. You could deal with a theme like this by detailing a single relationship, leading from friendship to love, or indeed from love to friendship – many true-life romances end up that way. However, the passion that is driving your story is the fact that someone whom you took to be a close and loyal friend has let you badly down, by offending against all the codes in which you believe. He has let his wife, or girlfriend, down too, but she does not see it that way. Why? Because love is blind and friendship is a more considered relationship.

We all have friends. We have all fallen in love. You are certainly writing about a topic of universal and enduring interest – but what is your premise? That love is blind? Partly, but that is only one aspect of your story. You are concerned by the values of friendship. *That* is your personal involvement. That is what is bugging you. That is your *motivation* and close friendships – male bonding, for example – can be just as strong as love ties: think of all the buddy movies you have ever seen.

The difference is that friendship is still rational, not like love, which is anything but reasoned or even reasonable. So to make your point, you need to write about two separate relationships: the one between you and your pal, and the one between him and her.

So, how are we going to launch the story? Not with the betrayal of trust. That must come as a denouement. First, it is necessary to establish the friendship. But you do not want this to be a close, domestic study. It is a feature film you want to write, not an episode for a soap (though the premise would serve equally well).

So you decide to select a large canvas, to tell an international story. Where should it be set? You may have been reading a book recently, about the immediate post-war years in Europe. It was a traumatic period, for civilians trying to re-build their lives, for soldiers who just wanted to get back home. It sounds like a good canvas for your picture.

Now the best way to describe a situation like this, for a cinema audience, is through the eyes of a stranger, so why not take your hero – who will also be the protagonist – and make him an American writer, say, because the US market likes American heroes and writers are reputed to be keen observers. Not a famous writer but someone you can relate to, like a guy who turns out cheap fiction – crime stories maybe, or westerns.

Where should the story be set – Paris, Budapest, Berlin, Vienna? All meet the requirements in different ways but the last two are better because they are at the time divided into sectors, providing a conflict between the Russians and the other Allies – the Iron Curtain is already beginning to be cranked down. Which of the two? Berlin has suffered the greatest destruction and consists largely of piles of rubble so Vienna might be the best choice. There is still some decent architecture standing and it is associated with lilting music. There is nothing like a good score to boost a film's performance. These commercial factors should not influence your story but there is no harm in bearing them in mind. Now one of the prime attributes of any protagonist is that he/she must never give up. If Lady Macbeth had been swayed by her husband, that would have been the end of the story, as it would have been had either Romeo or Juliet gone along with the wishes of their parents. There must always be hurdles to surmount and they must be cleared with relentless determination.

What will those obstacles be? Why does your hero go to Vienna? Just to see his old friend? But that would be the story of a friendship, not a betrayal, and you need the betrayal to prove the premise. So why not have a low-key but shock start – your hero has gone to Vienna to visit his buddy, who has offered him a job, only to find that the friend has died in a traffic accident? He goes to the funeral, tries to find out from his late pal's girl-friend, from his business associates, exactly what happened – but gets different stories from all of them. He begins to suspect the friend's death may not have been an accident at all.

In fact, he is getting so many varied accounts, he decides to stay in Vienna and find out the truth for himself. Everyone tries to tell him to leave it alone but the more they tell him, the more suspicious he gets, and the more steely his resolve to stay on – resolution is an essential ingredient of the make-up of any character who is the protagonist of the story.

But it is not so easy to stay, not without permission of the military authorities, who are unhelpful. A Major of the Military Police, in charge of the British sector, finds his presence a nuisance. The Major is pursuing an investigation into the black-market activities of the dead friend and another man, who has now gone missing. Perhaps the accident was no coincidence and was arranged by this man?

Your hero refuses to believe the major's accounts. He appeals to the dead man's girl-friend for information but she just shrugs off the accusations made against him. She is still in love with him, even though she has clearly been deceived herself. And love is blind.

When the dead man reveals himself as very much alive, the betrayal is complete. He makes light of his criminal dealings. It was just unfortunate that he got found out. And now he too wants the hero to leave Vienna. He has been asking too many awkward questions, drawing attention to something best forgotten.

But it is too late. The depth of the betrayal is all too clear. The enormity of the crimes committed cannot be sanctioned by an act of friendship. The protagonist can never give up, he must now report what he knows to the major. Besides, he is worried about the girl who has now had her (forged) papers taken away from her. In fact, he has fallen in love with her. He strikes a deal with the major to entrap the friend he had believed to be dead.

However, the criminal escapes. They comb the city for him. He has gone, literally, underground, giving us the opportunity for a protracted chase in the spectacular setting of the Vienna sewers – appropriately the home of the city's rats. The one-time close friend, now revealed as a vicious thug, is shot dead after having killed one of the pursuers himself. The final confrontation is of course with the hero.

The funeral that never was now really does take place. The major is there and our hero, who mourns the friend he used to have. And the girl-friend is there. She is heart-broken. Our hero tries to speak to her but she ignores him. No matter what he did, she still loves the man they have just buried. For her, it is the hero of the piece who is guilty of betrayal. But then, love is blind; friendship is rational. It depends on one's point of view. The premise is proved. In proving it, you have written a great movie.

If you did not spot it some pages back, it is the story of *The Third Man*. The film was directed by Carol Reed in 1949 and starred Joseph Cotton, Orson Welles, Trevor Howard and Alida Valli. The screenplay was by no less a master than the brilliant Graham Greene, England's finest novelist of the last century. It is one of the great classic movies. Every frame will hold your interest. It won many international awards. If you have not seen it, I urge you to do so. A brand new print was issued in 2000. Or get the video and study it. It is a lesson in film-making, in every respect. And you will need a knowledge of those other areas of film-making to be a good screenwriter. I cannot think of a more pleasurable or indulgent way to study your craft.

Here is a quick breakdown of another couple of fine films from that decade.

IT'S A WONDERFUL LIFE (1946)

Some films have *legs* and this one has long ones. It comes up on our television screens year after year, usually at Christmas time, and never seems to lose its appeal. Frank Capra taps into the emotional core of Mother America, or is sickeningly sentimental, whichever way you look at it, but people – ordinary people – love his films. The whimsical Capra touch was famous but irritating to some of his screenwriters.

Robert Riskin was reputed to have slapped down a hundred blank pages on the director's desk, saying: 'Here, Frank, put the Capra touch on that.'

The premise is pretty much in the title. The angel is the protagonist, who will not earn his wings unless he can convince James Stewart that his life really has been worthwhile. The greed of American corporate life provides the necessary antagonist. The conflict is almost between Stewart and his God, with a belief in the values of small town America as a substitute. Victim of a series of misfortunes, Stewart is unexpectedly edgy under pressure, giving a star performance that won him an Oscar nomination, though not a prize, as best actor.

Frank Capra is one of that rare breed of directors who create what is almost a *genre* of their own. Audiences flocked to see a Frank Capra film because they knew what the package was. It would be heart-warming, funny, well-acted, and have a message of optimism, a belief in the innate goodness of humanity – it had the Capra touch. *Film noir*, it is not.

THE MALTESE FALCON (1941)

Although no one used the term at the time, *The Maltese Falcon* is probably the archetype of the *film noir* genre. Based on a Dashiel Hammett novel, director John Huston cast Humprey Bogart as the laconic private eye, a role over which he would come to establish a near monopoly, until *The African Queen* anyway.

The cynicism, greed and betrayal that flood the film throughout, wash up nicely in the end with the usual premise of detective pictures, that crime does not pay and that truth will out. In the meantime, we have been entertained by a wonderful group of bizarre characters (played by Sidney Greenstreet, Peter Lorre et cetera,) playing out a marvelously Byzantine story. The protagonist was Sam Spade when he accepted the commission and the principal antagonist the Mary Astor character, who leads the conspiracy to make Sam the fall-guy.

The term 'classic' is not one that should be bestowed lightly, but this film qualifies in spades, forgiving the pun. The group of actors went on to form something of a repertory company, repeating their roles, proving the potency of gripping, well-defined characters in a screenplay. It is time we studied the importance of orchestrating a group of characters, for them to act in concert in a way that enables us to prove the premise of our story.

CHARACTER

I cannot underline enough the necessity for the protagonist to have determination. It can be expressed positively, like a detective's relentless pursuit of a killer, for example, or negatively, in stubbornness, a refusal to give in against all the odds, like the Western farmer's defense of his land against predatory cattle barons or a railway tycoon. Remember, if your protagonist should ever weaken in his or her resolve, then there will be no story; without conflict to sustain it, it will just peter out.

This determination must be matched by the aggression of the opponent, the antagonist, who need not be a single person. The antagonist can be a cartel of tobacco companies or pharmaceutical concerns – I leave you to identify them from some recent films – or a hostile grouping, like the families in *Romeo and Juliet* or the crooked trade-unionists in *On the Waterfront* – or even Fate, the indestructible entity in all the Greek tragedies. Oedipus may seek to challenge, but he can never escape, his destiny. Holly Martins' antagonist in *The Third Man*, constantly seeking by subterfuge to confuse and mislead him, was the long-time friend he had been mourning, Harry Lime himself. Othello is not the protagonist of the play but the antagonist, and a very dangerous one, of Iago, whose execution he could order at any time.

The terms *protagonist* and *antagonist* certainly suggest a conflict, and should provide one, but this does not necessarily take the form of a set-piece battle. It can be far more subtle than that. What motivates Rocky Balboa is his desire for recognition, not for beating to a pulp other fighters. At the end of the first film, during the big fight sequence, it does not matter any longer whether Rocky wins the match or not. What matters is that he has won the respect of the crowd in the hall, and of us in the audience.

Brutus and Anthony may be opponents in the field but neither is the protagonist. That role is fulfilled by Cassius, who organises the conspiracy to murder Caesar and thus sets into train all the events of Shakespeare's regal tragedy. It is the action contained within the premise that we are concerned with, not any battle, of wits or with weapons, that may be taking place on screen, though the two may be synchronised.

Protagonist and antagonist must be equally matched, at least for the final confrontation. More likely, the odds are stacked against the protagonist from the start. You might say that the protagonist can only be as compelling as he is driven to be by his opponent. It is the *intervention* that makes the protagonist what he or she is, the little person who, in the face of wickedness, says: 'I'm going to put a stop to this, whatever it takes.' The two have quite different sets of ethical principles which are irreconcilable, the point being that if either one were to weaken, the story would be over. The story must end with the defeat of one by the other, and the manner of the victory must be inherent in the premise.

Generally speaking, the antagonist's plan of action will already be effectively operating at the start of the picture when, by design or by chance, the protagonist discovers what that is, and decides he does not like it – more, that he is going to do something about it. To the villain of the piece, the intervention is no more than a minor irritation, a persistent fly to be squashed. Except this particular nuisance will *not* go away. Now he becomes even more of an irritant, he intrudes upon the antagonist's plans, thus forcing the villain to divert his energies to suppressing his opponent. At first, the struggle is unequal. Only a fool or someone of immense courage would stand up against such a powerful adversary (in comedy, like in *The General*, it sometimes is the fool). But we see our crusader gaining confidence and determination even in the face of seemingly impossible odds: we see him or her grow in stature. A character must have *growth*, there must be change – usually from pole to pole. As our protagonist grows, winning allies perhaps, so we see the might of the opponent gradually diminish. We never want the odds to be on the good guys winning: we do want to see them reduced to an even, or near even, chance. We must keep up the *conflict* at all times. We must keep the outcome uncertain. That uncertainty will always be in our minds. We know how often in real life the good guy loses out.

There will be more than two characters in your story, of course, and you will have to orchestrate your cast as a composer must his musical instruments. Every actor has a part to play and a contribution to make to the piece as a whole.

To pursue this analogy, of the film as a symphony or a concerto, the conductor is – must be – the director. But it is you, the writer, who has notated the entire score and arranged it for every single instrument, and it is that score which the director will now interpret for the audience. In Hollywood – or Rome, or London for that matter – you will find the director alters the notation, re-scores the instruments, calls *forte* where you have marked *piano* and plays the whole piece – parts of which he has probably re-written – at a different *tempo*.

Not even the most outrageous *maestro* would behave like this but literary works are different from musical ones. The fact is that what I have outlined above can, and does, happen. But this is the film business and if the literary score is not right, if the screenplay has strayed from its premise and lost its conflict, then these are matters which must be put right.

The hero/heroine does not always pursue a lonely furrow. Samuel Jackson's Marine Colonel in *Rules of Engagement* had Tommy Lee Jones's ex-Marine lawyer to help him out. Julia Roberts' Erin Brockovich had her boss, played by Albert Finney, who courageously put the resources of his law firm behind her at a critical moment in the fight. The other characters will tend to fall in place on either side of the conflicting parties, or may just sit on the fence – and their roles may be crucial when they decide to get off it.

No matter how excellent your premise, no matter how gripping the story in which you cloak it, the piece you are writing will not work unless your characters have life and growth. Indeed, there is no reason why you should not start with a character who intrigues you and then find the premise as a result of their actions. Character is the motivating power that drives the premise.

Suppose you had read in the newspaper an item about a woman who believed people were being poisoned by noxious chemical deposits and was mounting an attack on the giant pharmaceutical companies who produced them? Now that is a promising start to a story. You have yet to find your premise but you can see the conflict and you can imagine the kind of feisty young woman who would embark on such a course. It is her character that entices you, that motivates you to inquire further and see whether all the elements for a scenario are there. What was her name again? Ah, Erin Brockovich.

This lady had a passion for justice, in real life as well as on the screen. She believed that respect for fellow human beings was more important than making piles of money. It gave her life a meaning, a purpose. It was the premise for her actions. She was a character with whom any audience could sympathise, even relate. She was poor and she was struggling but she could not be written off as trailer trash: she had intelligence and she had spirit and she had pride.

Premise, protagonist, antagonist. The story needs only the orchestration of its characters, on either side of the conflict, to have all the elements of a solid structure. *Erin Brockovich* is an object lesson in scenario construction, containing all those principles of good writing which we are discussing. If you have not seen the film, get a video or DVD and see it now.

When we go to the cinema or to the theatre, we go to see a reflection of ourselves. Nothing is more attractive to us than the antics of the human race. We go to see characters with whom we can identify. We want to see them run the gamut of emotions which we ourselves have experienced or hope to experience at some time; we have all felt affection, love, passion, obsession, as we have unease, dislike, hate, fear, even disgust. Our feelings have many times ranged from optimism to pessimism, or conversely from despair to elation. We have all known loyalty, faith, generosity, happiness but also misery, betrayal, vindictiveness. The list is endless and it comprises the human condition which, whether we are conscious of it or not, is a perpetual obsession – it is, after all, life.

For us to be impressed with your characters onscreen, we need to know them, and for us to do that it is essential that you not only have this knowledge yourself but are able to communicate it to us – everything about them. However, in a dramatic piece you will not always know your characters intimately unless you are writing about your parents, your siblings, or your best friends.

That selection alone would inevitably limit you. There might be one dramatic story to be culled from your home environment – there usually is, since most authors write an autobiographic work at some time in their lives. But, unless you were surrounded by some pretty bizarre characters – as Eugene O'Neill was, for example – there will probably be only one. Remember you are writing fiction and it is not in the detail and the fact – these are matters for journalists or documentary-makers – but in your imagination that you will find your stories and your characters.

But all imagination is based on experience. You cannot create a character out of pure imagination except perhaps in the realm of science fiction which, by definition, is not reality. For your film to be successful you must portray characters that are real – or that seem to the audience to be real. And audiences know. They may not, as a mass, be able to voice their reasons for thinking so, but they know from their own knowledge of the world whether your characters are real or fake.

Some fake characters do work, but only in the genre known as hokum. James Bond is a fake. We know nothing about him other that that he is a well-educated man in the employ of the Secret Service, possessing insatiable sexual urges and good luck beyond all reason. Plus a license to kill, of which he takes considerable advantage.

The formula was one that needed no premise other than that the forces of good will always defeat the forces of evil, not that there is anything wrong with that. Stories based on that premise have been written for centuries, beginning with the mediaeval morality plays. It is a premise in which we believe because we want to believe it. We know there are dark forces out there and we are afraid of them but we know that God – or some other cosmic being – in His heaven will always protect us. It is the premise of *Star Wars*, of any *Dracula* film, probably of any horror film ever conceived.

It is not a finite battle of course: the struggle will continue. You may defeat the killer-bug and save the world but the last words of your film will be that another has been discovered in Seattle. Dracula will arise from his grave. Satan will always be around but so will God, to frustrate his many and various acts of malevolence. There are a thousand stories.

The antagonist in any James Bond film is Ernst Blofeld, or an *alter ego*. He (has there been a she?) has already decided on a plan to dominate the world or decimate its population and James Bond (in his various reincarnations) is called upon to save us. The basic plot-line is as simple as that – always. Just as Eric Brockovitch stood up to the chemical giants, so James Bond, showing courage (and not a little *chuzpah*) beyond the call of duty, takes on the greed of the power-hungry, multi-national, mega-buck corporations typified by the crazed Blofeld.

The Bond films are tremendous fun. They probably cost upward of $100 million dollars to make these days and so the production values are always great. A sizeable portion of that budget has probably gone on the opening sequence, which is invariably audacious and breathtaking, the perfect teaser for the story which follows.

We know the end already – in the sense we know that Bond will win through (and get the girl) – but we don't care. We want the arch-villain to be destroyed in his lair and, when the denouement comes, we want it to be as spectacular as possible. So somehow regiments of baddies armed with the latest weaponry fire off millions of rounds of ammunition but fail to curb the incredible exploits of our super-hero.

During the course of the film, Bond's life will have been on the line on numerous occasions, giving rise to some magnificent action sequences. There will have been a deal of smart, wise-cracking dialogue with plenty of sly double-entendres, even in the face of seemingly certain death, and several sexual encounters with scantily clad, beautiful (and bountiful) girls.

Incredible, one must add, is the operative word. It is actually quite silly that Bond never gets hit by any single one of the millions of bullets (not to mention more powerful missiles) fired in his direction. Miraculously they all end exactly two inches either in front of, or behind him. The girl accompanying him is equally blessed. I sometimes think wistfully: if only he could at least stub his toe!

What James Bond does not have is any recognisable form of growth, and it is the development of our characters which make them seem real.

There will be a great temptation for you to people your script with characters you have gleaned from all the films you have seen – including James Bond. Fight against it. It may not be apparent to you but it will be to the shrewd reader if your script is a hotchpotch of other films. James Bond must be the character most drawn upon, usually accompanied by what the author imagines is slick dialogue – also based on the Bond films. The individual scenes may come from other sources – Tarantino is much copied.

Love scenes are often ludicrous, sketched from the writer's perhaps fertile, but quite unconvincing, imagination. Do not succumb to it. It is much better to write about people and events you know. Yet there is no reason why you should not get your initial inspiration from a film you have seen – preferably, an extension of the idea, rather than just copying it – or from a news report. Its effect on you is all part of your experience.

The problem is that because so many people today have grown up watching television, they tend to assume this is the obvious medium in which to write, and it can indeed be a rewarding occupation, both professionally and financially – if you get enough work.

But there is also a tendency to create, or re-create, the very same characters you have been watching. There is a startlingly common belief that all policemen behave as they do in *The Bill*, and that all doctors and nurses – and the running of the National Health Service – are exactly like their portrayal in *Casualty*.

These are both excellent, long-running series, which I am sure are meticulously researched. But the reality, if you are unfortunate enough to find yourself in either a hospital or a police-station, is almost certainly very different. There is a good reason for this. Drama is the essence, rather than a representation, of life. True life is documentary footage although even that can be highly selective, or slanted through the editing process, or just prone to dramatic license.

It is not easy to get away from these norms. If you are invited to write for *The Bill* or any other television series, there is a basic format of storytelling which has served them well and provides continuity. That format is inclined to be fairly rigid because, as television has become wall-to-wall entertainment, just a product to fill the screen for a finite period, so shooting schedules have been cut to the bone in order to achieve a quick, economic turn-around. The regular characters are all clearly delineated and have become known to the public which, sadly, in the main suffers from collective couch-potato syndrome, and would not want to see anything that was demanding or unfamiliar. But do not be fazed by this and remember that even within a rigid format, a good strong premise can still make a point not made before. There will always be *outside* characters with which you can make a mark – think of some of the traffic passing through the station in *NYPD Blue* – and there may also be the opportunity of exploring one or more of the running characters in more depth than usual.

Writing is all about observation: it is the observer's point of view set down, but that point of view needs to be essential. What people do from hour to hour, the minutiae of their existence, tends to be extremely boring if recorded in detail, even when engaged in exciting activity. The exciting part takes only a fraction of the time available. Even if you want to show a *boring* character, you must do it brilliantly, humorously, or it will be just that.

Think Mike Leigh, particularly some of his earlier films. The characters are laid back, inarticulate, leading immensely dreary lives, mostly moving through entirely predictable situations. Yet we empathise with them, laugh at them, care for them – and all because we feel we know them, because they are so real in their awkwardness, their inability to express themselves. Somehow Leigh turns that awkwardness into a kind of grace and that inarticulateness into a kind of lyricism.

How does he do it? Leigh's particular genius lies in encouraging the observational talents of his cast. From a basic idea they will spend literally months studying all the traits of the characters they will play, rehearsing and improvising until the director is ready to shoot the picture, when the results of all that hard work make it look so easy. Not everyone will be granted such indulgence. Leigh devised his own way of working in the theatre and after some huge successes, carried it forward into film-making. But however you work, the focus must be on the character, rather than the plot. With good characters, good stories arise naturally.

If you do not have an interest in people, you will never be a creative writer. Study your family, your friends, your work-mates, your colleagues, as closely as you can without causing them embarrassment. Observe your fellow passengers on the bus, the people you pass in the street. Take a look at Mayfair as well as Brixton, at Shoreditch and Southall. Go out into the suburbs, the provinces, visit Europe, travel as widely as you can. Just observe and absorb, let it all sink in. Make notes, by all means, keep a scrapbook if you like. But it is your brain which will store and sift your observations and convert them one day into the imagery that will allow you to write a gem-like short story, a fine novel or a superb screenplay. The proper study of mankind is man.

Before we recap what we have learned so far, let us study the evolution of film a little more, this time looking at the 1950s, a period of considerable progress in the art of the scenario.

RASHOMON (1950)

This was the film that brought one of the world's great film-makers, Akira Kurosawa, to the attention of the West and, indeed, probably popularised Japanese films here. Hitherto, they had been confined to cinema-goers of somewhat esoteric taste.

The film asks the great philosophical question: 'What is truth?' The premise is the answer: that we all have our own individual concepts. The story is straightforward: a forest bandit kills a samurai and rapes his wife, the scene being witnessed by a woodcutter. The telling of the story is anything but straightforward and indeed lifted the art of the scenario to a new and sophisticated level.

The four characters of the scene then re-enact it for us, each from their own point of view. No one is objective, of course. Each story seems to be tinged with fantasy, telling us more about the characters themselves than it does about the event. Who should we believe? Do we even know ourselves, what is truth?

This fascinating picture, which won a Special Award at the Oscar ceremonies for being the outstanding foreign language film, is an absolute must to see for any aspiring screenwriter. At a length of only 88 minutes, in black and white, it is a little masterpiece.

If you cannot get to see it on the big screen, see it whichever way you can, but do not miss it.

THE SEVENTH SEAL (1956)

Like *Rashomon*, *The Seventh Seal* proved to us that the cinema is a universal art and, more, does not entirely rely upon the English language. It also introduced us to another world-class director, Ingmar Bergman. Within a year he had also presented to us *Wild Strawberries* and comprehensively established himself as a master film-maker.

It won no Oscar nominations, perhaps because of its bleakness, and there was no rush by Hollywood to sign up this brilliant new star in the firmament. The basic requirement for American films was still that they should be escapist entertainment and this was anything but that. The epitome of the *art film* and, as such, joyfully lampooned by *Monty Python* and many others – including Woody Allen who later was quite seriously inspired by the director – it remains a study of doom.

The premise is that man must hold to his faith and come to terms with his God. Set in a mediaeval landscape, ravaged by the Black Death, its people near demented, the story is of a quest for truth (again) and the protagonist is the knight returned from the Crusades travelling through this nightmare country he no longer recognises as his own. The images of self-flagellation, burning witches, the chess-game with Death, are memorable. They are like early religious paintings, brought to the screen and to life. The scenes of the plague are reminiscent of what the world might be like in a Doomsday scenario. This is not a film one can easily get out of one's mind. Indeed, it is something more than a film: it is an experience. Having seen it, you will never quite be the same.

Do not aspire to write like it. If you want to model yourself on Bergman, *Wild Strawberries* would be a better choice. That did win a Best Screenplay nomination.

RECAP

Let us go back over what we have discussed so far.

- Write *about* something, make a statement, select a premise and then set out to prove it.

- Choose your *protagonist*, the character who will drive the premise through to a satisfactory end.
- Then select an *antagonist* who will not only provoke the *conflict* which is so vital, but seek to repulse or deflect any opposition, with brutality if necessary.
- Remember *neither side can back down*. Each must have in their own mental make-up a grit and determination that ensures the conflict will continue until the premise is proved.
- *Orchestrate your characters* carefully, keeping the balance of conflict even, when it counts. It does not have to be even to start with, it can be ill-balanced, unfair, unjust. It can be one person fighting a megalithic company but that one character will grow in strength though there may be many setbacks – and will sap the opposing side's will to succeed.
- *Remember all the characters must make their own individual contributions*. Whether they have small roles or important ones, unless they fit into the story, the jigsaw will not be completed. Do not leave holes!
- Your story does not have to be directly in your experience but it will be real and truthful if you can match your experience against it. *The same has to apply to characters*. They have a function and will be an amalgam of people you know, given the traits and the motivation necessary to fulfil that function.
- *Look and learn but do not copy*! What filters through your mental processes will become original but that filtration must take place. Be honest and straightforward. In particular, be honest with yourself.

CHARACTER AGAIN – NOTHING MATTERS MORE

Before we move on, let us discuss character in more detail. I ask you to draw a box for me. You pencil out a square. It does not look like a box. It looks like a square. What does it lack? It lacks perspective. It is two-dimensional: it has height and width, but no depth. When we give it depth, it looks like a box, or like a cube, anyway. We can make the cube anything we like: a box, a house, one of a pair of dice. It still needs the detail, the shading, to make it an individual object, with its own character, but it has body now. It has a third dimension. Your characters need to be tri-dimensional for us to accept that they are real, to believe in them, but what is it that gives our characters body and depth?

Let us deconstruct a human being. What is he or she all about? We could start with the obvious question – male or female – though even that is a category which may be refined. Someone born a man could have been surgically altered to become a woman. Another person could have a man's mind and mentality trapped in a woman's body. When one considers a character's sexuality, the possibilities are endless. Straight, gay, lesbian? Virile, impotent? Cross-dresser, paedophile, sadist, transvestite, masochist? Our sexuality is a dominant influence on our character, both internally and externally.

So is our appearance. Will your character be tall, thin, fat, minute? What colour skin? Handsome, ugly, of average appearance? Dark-haired, blonde, or a red-head? Clear-skinned, or scarred with acne? Hirsute? Clean-shaven? Are the features regular or lop-sided? Are there distinguishing marks or traits? Again, the possibilities are endless. What we need to know is that our physical appearance is important, it helps shape our lives.

If you are simply describing the commissionaire who opens the taxi door for you outside a swish hotel – and that is his role in the film, no more – then his appearance is immaterial so long as it does notice. Commissionaires are generally tall, imposing figures, usually ex-army, and if you cast someone like that, he will go unnoticed but still add authenticity to the picture you present. If he is a dwarf, on the other hand, then he will certainly have been noticed and you may have taken the audience's eye off the ball. They will start questioning the meaning of this bizarre figure when there may be none, other than to open the taxi door. This may be all right in a David Lynch film but what we want is for the audience to follow the progress of the man in the taxi, and we do not want to divert from this.

A tall man can appear more confident but the height can cause a postural slump. A small man tends to be upright, reaching to be level, brash perhaps as he over-compensates for his lack of stature. A beautiful woman can knock you out with the way she looks, until you realise there is no one in upstairs, the lights are out. Physical beauty is no substitute for intelligence, warmth, personality. And these attributes in a plain girl can transform her appearance and radiate an inner beauty to stunning effect.

Physical appearance can also be important in defining the motivation of the character. There is no point in describing a tall, blonde, Adonis-like man as the kind of actor to portray *The Hunchback of Notre Dame* or *The Phantom of the Opera* – it just will not work. Their lives were shaped by their disfigurements.

The physical appearance of our players may not be important but they must look right – which is not to say that they must be clichéd. Not all heroes are six feet tall, especially if they are played by Mel Gibson or Tom Cruise. Not all romantic heroines are beautiful.

But you have to ask whether the age, the weight, the colour of hair and eyes, are right for the characters you are describing, that their physical appearance is *consistent* with the story you are telling. Whether someone is bald or hairy, their posture and physical defects – hereditary or otherwise – all combine to make a single individual being, whose presence will blend perfectly into the larger scheme which is your screenplay.

However, it is what lies *behind* the physical exterior that is probably more important to us, and to the story. What level of education do the characters have, and what degree of intelligence (the two are not necessarily the same)? What kind of work do they do and what are their hobbies; what kind of sports do they play? Are they healthy? Do they suffer from asthma, insomnia, Parkinson's disease, osteoporosis? Are they HIV positive? Do they have full-blown AIDS?

There are darker inner areas. Some of your characters may be given to depression or paranoia. Others might be claustrophobic, agoraphobic, or suffer from vertigo, and all these fears and inner tensions will affect their demeanour, their thoughts and words and actions. What kind of disposition do they have? Are they gentle, kind, outgoing? Or rude, angry, overbearing? And remember, the outward display does not always reflect the inner truth. Attitudes can be affected to disguise secret fears and compulsions, which may not even be consciously known.

We cannot get into a two-year psychoanalysis programme in order to know our characters in the most intimate detail but we must know what makes them tick. We do know that Freud, Jung, Adler and others clearly believe that it is the inner self that motivates us, far more powerfully than any external influences.

Not that these are unimportant. We are not just the product of our genes, or our traumas – we are also shaped by our environment. Poverty might well be the engine of our motivation to achieve whatever aims we have. Real and imagined slights are great motivators, the powerful chips we carry on our shoulders. Class makes a big difference. Modern progressive democracies claim to be classless societies but that is not true. The rich still get richer and the poor, by comparison anyway, poorer.

THE SOCIAL BACKGROUND – ENVIRONMENT

What is the character's background? Where does he or she come from? From Beneden and Girton; from Eton, Magdalene and the Guards; or from a housing estate in Peckham? What is his class, his family environment?

You cannot go merely by appearances: it was the same Michael Caine who played the Cockney wide boy in *Alfie* who also played the aristocratic young infantry officer in *Zulu*. You judged him from his bearing, his dress, his accent – all of which may be adopted, of course – again like Michael Caine in *Dirty Rotten Scoundrels.*

There is, and there will continue to be, a class structure (anywhere) which affects the opportunities available for work, for culture, for education and even for health. Immigration may give us a richer, more diverse, multi-cultural society but it also results in inner-city ghettos which will be prisons for their inhabitants – including some white natives – for the rest of their lives. Society, not any particular government, has allowed the growth of an under-class. You need to understand these niceties in order to know the world you live in, the world you are going to write about unless your bag is science fiction – and even out there, there are parallels.

Is the class-structure rigid? Not at all. Is there upward mobility? Certainly. There are always examples of those who have climbed from the bottom to the very top of the ladder. But why and how did they do that? And why and how were all those others condemned to crowd, cowed, at the base? Remember, life at the top is often transitory. As you mount each rung, do not step on the fingers of those whom you may meet again, coming down (a useful premise, in itself).

The answers will be found in the various traits of human beings that have already been mentioned and the many other aspects of character that are yet to be explored. Parental influence is tremendously important, as is lack of such influence. A child learns from its parents or carers, often adopting their characteristics, their choices, their prejudices – even their bestiality.

The marital influence can be equally strong and the duties of parenthood create previously unknown disciplines, to which we react in different ways, some beneficial, some not. Children are loved and nurtured. They are also tortured and murdered. Abuse in the home can mark a child for life. Marriage effects a change in status, often with consequences. It gives a stability, not always blissful. For some, it is a life sentence, a loss of freedom. The ubiquitous mortgage can be a ball-and-chain. Some are happy, others live in misery. Wife-beating, even in these days of sexual equality, is rife. What inner terror, what sense of shame, prevents victims from breaking out of their incarceration?

Our peers are always a major influence in our lives. We unite with friends – often life-long ones – at school, university, in the streets, or our working environment. We join groups, we stray in packs, we form and we break off relationships. We are often envious of others, or jealous of them. We enter into collusions, conspiracies, to do someone down, in order to obtain promotion perhaps, or better ourselves, or just to survive in the jungles of commerce, industry or academia.

Our actions are informed by our beliefs, our education in the wider, not the formal sense. We may be religious by upbringing or by personal choice. We may adopt a philosophy. We may teach others or we may not have the ability, or the inclination, to pass on our knowledge. Most sad of all, we may have none to give.

It is not only where you live, where you go to school, what your father's job may be. There is a wider context, outside the town or borough where you live, outside this country, this continent. Where there is cause there is effect, be it economic, political or ecological. You all know about the destruction of the rain-forests, about global warming. Remember John Donne's prophetic warning – *No man is an island*!

Our lives are largely shaped by others, by events outside our control. We may turn out to be good, or bad; generous or mean-spirited; rich or poor. The fates and our own freedom of will are the determining factors, and the two may clash. What is certain is that we will all be individual human beings and the actions of even the most humble of us will have some effect on the world in which we live. We are all characters in a play, a film, a story called *Life*.

The more we know about our characters, the more real they will be. Are they rich or poor, and to what degree? What are their occupations, religion, race? What are their hobbies: how do they find recreation? What are their interests – politics, spiritualism, sports, necromancy? Nothing defines human beings more than the environmental factors of their upbringing. The class struggle, at any level, is endless, varying only in its subtlety or brutality. Be sure your characters have the social background necessary for them to perform their roles with conviction. There should be no false notes. The ears of an audience are keenly tuned.

It is their transparent validity which will make your screenplay stand out from so many others. The very first hurdle you have to surmount is getting whoever is reading the script to recommend it, and then whoever makes the decisions to select it for development. A director will then have to be found for it and you want your script to be picked out from the pile of others he/she is probably considering. Having survived thus far, the script will still have to prove itself as being attractive to leading actors (and to good actors in the supporting roles), otherwise the picture might never get made, however powerful or ingenious the story. There still needs to be a plus factor and that is the strength of your characterisation. It is your characters who will sell the film, at practically every stage, so know them well. Know them intimately.

It is worth writing a one-page biography on each of your principal characters unless you feel you know them well enough for it to be unnecessary. But you will be surprised, when you check your draft screenplay against the biographical notes, how much important detail you have passed over.

Select your characters for whatever job they have to do in the script. The protagonist's background – probably their whole lives – may have been leading up to this moment, as have the lives and backgrounds of the characters who jointly comprise the antagonist. Whatever the conflict may be, neither of them will ever throw in the towel. This is essential. Battles must be won or lost. Premises must have conclusions. You will need to orchestrate each and every one of your players so that they are all in tune with your premise.

Another essential is that, in the course of your story, your characters must change. They must grow or diminish. They must develop. Change is a natural process. Life is change. Where there is no change, there is only death. But even a dead body changes. It decomposes, food for worms. Or incinerates. Ashes to ashes, dust to dust. Change is action. Action is life. Every day we act and re-act, as do those who people our lives. There is constant movement. Nothing is ever still. We talk about 'the quick and the dead'. Quick means in action, undergoing a process of change. Change indicates life. When you write your screenplay (or play, or novel, or short story), you are going to tell a tale, you are going to outline a change in situation, a change in the characters you are using to portray that situation. If there were no change, then there would be no interest. Some examples follow.

ERIN BROCKOVICH (2000)

The multi-national company has polluted an area of land to the detriment of the health of the people living on it. If there are any complaints, they buy them off. There are no moral issues so far as the company is concerned: this is just hard-nosed business. But there is a moral issue for Erin, played by Julia Roberts. She feels she represents those downtrodden little people and she wants them to fight back, as she does.

To the company she is just a jumped-up little clerk from a law office. But Erin is David and she intends to slay Goliath. The *situation changes* from one of impregnability for the company to doubt, to panic, to surrender. Conversely, Erin blooms in confidence. Sick of being regarded as trailer trash, she finds a role for herself as champion of the underdog. She will *never* give up. She may be poor but she has pride. Her hard upbringing has made her a tough opponent. She grows and wins the respect of her boss, the gratitude of the people she has helped. She *achieves* something. She bursts the inflated balloon of the company's arrogance. We all want the little man/woman to win.

THE THIRD MAN (1949)

Holly Martins, the character played by Joseph Cotton, has always had a dog-like devotion to Harry Lime, an old friend and schoolboy hero. A not-very-successful writer, when Harry offers him a job in Vienna, he leaves immediately, but at a bad time for Harry, who suddenly finds himself the top suspect in a nasty case of black-marketing drugs. *The situation has changed.*

You will not see every single aspect of your story appear in the movie. Inevitably there is a *back story* which has influenced the plot and affected its characters. In the back story which precedes *The Third Man*, Harry has stage-managed an accident, in which he supposedly dies. So Holly arrives in time to go to the funeral where he meets a British major, commanding that sector of Vienna, and Harry's girlfriend. No one tells Holly the real background; the major is still not satisfied about the circumstances surrounding Harry's death. Holly asks questions but gets only evasive answers. For him, as a writer, the story does not add up. He persists, even when everyone urges him to leave Vienna. And he falls in love with the Alida Valli character, although she still loves Harry. Before the famous denouement in the city's sewers, Holly's perception of Harry has changed from that of hero to sick gangster. The writer's natural romanticism is confronted by harsh reality. He learns that although love may be blind, friendship is not immutable. He goes back to America a sadder, wiser man. All that glitters is not gold.

THE NECESSITY OF CHANGE

Every human being is in a state of constant fluctuation. Nothing on earth is static and certainly not its inhabitants. To return to our musical metaphor, we are like stringed instruments, vibrating, changing pitch or key. We interplay with others and produce sweet music or a cacophony of sound.

Change can be internal or external or both. You woke up today a different person from the one you were yesterday. You may be unaware of it but you added to your experience, you learned something. You interacted with others. You were pleased or angry or depressed or hopeful. Maybe you loved or hated. Maybe you humiliated someone or were humiliated yourself. But you changed. You were changed yourself and your actions, in some small way, changed the world about you.

It is vital that in the process of telling your story, your characters change. They have to prove your premise in the same way that a series of letters and numerals proves a logical or mathematical theorem. If they are to make a positive statement, it must weigh against a negative of the same proposition. Your characters will effect change and in doing so must themselves change. They grow, they diminish, they win, they lose, they pass through a series of interactions and, above all, they learn. Art is what teaches us about life. It shows us how to look differently at a subject. It illuminates a path for us. We go to an art gallery, a play, the opera or the ballet, to the cinema, to learn. To be entertained as well, certainly, in the same way that a well-taught lesson might also entertain us, but deep down it is to learn, to grow a little ourselves by the enrichment of our experience.

We all of us want change in our lives. We want to grow, we want to improve ourselves. Not just to be rich, own a Ferrari, shop at Harrods, wear Versace – but to be popular, respected, admired and, most of all, to be loved. Some of us achieve all, or some of those aims. Most of us do not. We have to make do with dreams, with the products of our imagination. But we can draw imagination from others, whom we see in the movies, who do change their lives, who defeat injustice, who find love.

To every story there is a beginning and an end. Too obvious? Do not believe it. We are talking technically here. You are writing about something; you are stating a premise and premises entail conclusions. Conclusions follow logically from premises so let us think in terms of conclusions rather than endings. Ending are often pat, contrived – they can even be a total cop-out.

I did an editing job on a play once. It had been turned down by a series of managements but one optimist thought it might be put right. He was wrong. A court-room drama, it had a terrible curtain-line, with the judge asking the jury whether the leading character was guilty or not guilty. As the foreman of the jury opened his mouth, so the curtain fell. It was risible. I almost declined the job on the spot but the author was a very famous novelist whose name would mean something on the marquee, and I was tempted to be part of the action in what would never be a very good play but could be a successful one. So I took it to pieces, searched for the heart of the play, which was not the trial but a love story. Then, immediately, everything fell into place. I accepted the assignment and after giving it a premise which changed the emphasis of the story, re-jigging the dialogue, clearly establishing the premise and having the jury deliver a verdict, the play worked – as a love story. That was the basis of the success of Jeffrey Archer's West End hit *Beyond Reasonable Doubt*.

If the author had any doubt about the value of my contribution, which I am sure he did, it should have been clear to him when his next play *Exclusive*, presumably a solo effort, folded within a few weeks. He is nothing if not determined, however, if perhaps a bit foolhardy. Yet another effort reached the West End stage after this, on this occasion starring the author, which blindly tried to prove yet again that asking the audience to deliver a verdict is a stunning *coup de théatre*. It is not, it is just a game-show gimmick, and the play was another flop. Only you, the writer, can prove your own premise: you cannot leave it to others.

Endings on their own, as opposed to conclusions, are mechanical. They are the hero riding off into the setting sun, or walking along the long straight road that leads to nowhere and everywhere; or the happy marriage, love sealed with a kiss; the triumph over adversity in a court of law, or on the football field, or any other sports concourse. They are vengeance, the murderer who is sentenced, the bad guy shot in a duel, the bright hope for the future, heavenly choirs, the stake through the heart of the vampire.

They can be ironic, of course: the creature just born in Seattle, the hand coming out of the grave in *Carrie*, the happiness of the man who has just killed his friend in the French film *Harry, He Is Here To*

Help. Remember a proposition is that which is asserted and it can be true or false. What is important is that it leads to a logical and satisfying conclusion. Then, true or false, uplifting or ironic, spiritual or cynical, it hits home.

Let us, continuing our brief interludes of cinematic history, check on two films of the 1960s with great endings.

PSYCHO (1960)

It is difficult not to describe *Psycho* as a masterpiece, even though it has its faults. The protagonist is clearly the character played by Janet Leigh, whom we see embezzle funds from her employer and then make a quick escape. She is an attractive and interesting young woman and we are intrigued by what may be her story. But we never find out. About a third of the way through the picture, she is shockingly murdered in the shower, at the motel where she has pulled in for the night. The conflict she has provoked is not that provided by a criminal investigation into her flight, but a murder hunt.

The shower scene is probably the most famous in the history of cinema, along with the pram clattering down the steps in *Battleship Potemkin*, and the violence is all imagined. We see only the knife slashing at the curtain and the blood spiralling down the sink-hole. There are other scenes which everyone who has seen the film cannot fail to remember: the whooping dervish attacking the detective on the stairs, the mummified corpse in the rocking chair.

There are innumerable false trails and misleading clues, but these are all part of Hitchcock's repertoire. It was not a big-budget picture, indeed its primary purpose was to be shown on television. The first preview changed all that. Word of mouth and a clever advertising campaign did the rest.

It is *not* an example of great screenplay writing but of great direction, an object lesson in the manipulation of an audience by the juxtaposition of images, and the startling use of sound. It is a brilliant display of the conjurer's art, deceiving us constantly, guiding us firmly away from the denouement so that when it comes it is brutal and shocking – even unforgettable.

You might write another *Psycho* but I doubt it – many others have tried and failed. There have been *sequels* and a *prequel* but they just trade on the names of Norman Bates and his motel. Homage to the master abounds but there is only one original. To this day I am convinced that I saw it the first time in colour but that was my imagination – it is in black and white. It won no Oscars but there were nominations for Alfred Hitchcock and Janet Leigh. No one remembers the credit on the screenplay. It was Joseph Stefano from the book by Robert Bloch.

See it tonight – if you dare.

LAWRENCE OF ARABIA (1962)

No apologies for citing another picture by David Lean, undoubtedly the foremost British director of the last century. I knew David: we were members of the same union, the Association of Cinema and Television Technicians. As President, I represented the union at David's memorial service. Most people found him distant but, surprisingly, he was actually shy.

The canon of his films is remarkable but it is probably *Lawrence of Arabia* for which he will be principally remembered. An awesomely expensive film, it had no stars at the time – Peter O'Toole and Omar Sharif were comparatively unknown. There was a good back-up of top actors, however, for the many cameo roles. But it is the desert which is the star, the vast canvas of undulating yellow – we all remember the little speck of black, an image shimmering in the heat like a swirling wave, as Sharif galloped towards camera and unforgettably introduced himself.

The film is based on T. E. Lawrence's autobiographical work *The Seven Pillars of Wisdom*, in which he tells how he led the Arab revolt against the Turks in the First World War. As such it is a fascinating slice of history but the story Lean tells is about the man himself, his inner conflicts, his indefatigable courage – and his ultimate rejection by both the Arabs and the British authorities. If ever there was an outsider, it was Lawrence. Lawrence, the protagonist, when a junior officer, comes up with the idea of taking Aquaba from the Turks, who were allied to the Germans. On a secret reconnaissance trip to Dera, he is caught and emotionally and physically abused. The Turks are undoubtedly the villains. The premise is that a man can make his dreams come true but there will always be a price to pay: that was certainly the case with Lawrence.

Although described by the *New York Times'* critic as being 'as devoid of humanity as the parched desert sands', the film won seven Oscars, including one for best music (Maurice Jarre). The writer, on the other hand, the admirable Robert Bolt, did not even get a nomination.

ANOTHER MEMOIR

At the beginning of the 1970s, Rome was no longer the centre of American production in Europe and, when I got back to London, there was very little happening here either. About the only company making films was Hammer. With two friends, I started a production company called Fantale Films and we managed to make four pictures in less than two years, which was more than MGM had made down the road at its Boreham Wood studios.

Censorship was in rapid decline and there was no longer a Lord Chamberlain to dictate morality in the theatre. My principal creative contribution to cinema so far was the invention of hand-touch sex in *Barbarella*, but *The Vampire Lovers*, based on a short story *Carmilla* by Sheridan Le Fanu, allowed me to create the first nude, lesbian vampires, and a picture which I little thought at the time would be another cult success. We made two others for Hammer, *Twins of Evil* and *Lust for a Vampire*, and would probably have gone on making them till this day but for the retirement of James Carreras. His son

Michael took over and shifted the company into a completely different direction. It did not work and Hammer has remained pretty dormant as a production company ever since, although they are always announcing new plans. Under new management, these might take shape. Our three Hammer films have been dubbed *The Karnstein Trilogy* by the aficionados – there are millions of them, worldwide – and I am still forever getting invitations to fantasy film festivals.

The Eady Levy existed then, a subsidy arranged by the government funded by a tax on box-office receipts, which was particularly generous for low-budget film-makers. We had wound up Fantale by then and I was keen to produce on my own, and perhaps direct. With the old Hammer production line at a halt, the only other low-budget pictures being made were sex-comedies, which were making a lot of money. It was also fun, being in the front line, and I was pleased to be giving a break to a lot of young technicians. My assistant was Martin Campbell and I gave him his first picture to direct. He also directed *Three for All*, a musical, which I produced for Dick James with Harold Shampan. Martin went on to greater things and is now a big-time Hollywood director. His last three credits, as I write, are *GoldenEye*, *Mask of Zorro* and *Vertical Limit*, which cost more than $100 million dollars – without stars!

I also wrote a screenplay with director Anthony Simmons called *The Optimists of Nine Elms*, which starred Peter Sellers, a very curious man. Simmons had, a few years ago, written and directed *Four in the Morning*, a stunning example of indigenous, gritty realism. And I toured Australia and New Zealand, directing in the theatre.

If it was pretty quiet here at that time – it was all happening in America. 1972 saw the first of the Godfather films and in 1975 Steven Spielberg established himself with *Jaws*. A new breed of film-makers had emerged with the big studios acting more as publishing houses, financing and distributing independent pictures. Others were engaging themselves in the bread-and-butter business of television production. It was the period when the multiple sequel was invented for *Jaws*, *Halloween*, *Friday the 13th* and *Nightmare on Elm Street* – those new-look horror creations that made the old Hammer product seem very tame – though it still endures. The decade had started with two smash hits, *M*A*S*H*, made by that marvellous director, Robert Altman, who also shot *Nashville* in 1975, and *Love Story*, an unexpected success. I worked with Arthur Hiller, the director, in Rome and have since met him many times at occasions hosted by the Directors' Guild of America. We agreed that every year has its *Love Story* (in which he had points, making him a very rich man). Subsequently, in the UK, we had similar successes with *Four Weddings and a Funeral* and *The Full Monty*, modest films which still drew countless millions at the box office. Incidentally, if you ever get points yourself, you will find that the millions really are countless – no one seems able to count them properly, not your share anyway. You would be amazed if I told you the names of some smash-hit films where the points-holders never received a penny – not for years at least.

George Lucas directed *Star Wars* and produced the Indiana Jones movies (all of them in the UK!). Other star talents to emerge were Martin Scorsese, John Carpenter and Brian de Palma. For the Americans, it was an exciting period of change and invention. For the UK, it was still the same pattern, mostly dreary domestic output while at the same time we were making great films – like *Cabaret* for example – but for the USA.

Moving on...

ORCHESTRATING YOUR CHARACTERS

We have dealt with the central figures, the protagonist and the antagonist, but there will obviously be more than two characters involved in the conflict. *Rocky* was not just about Rocky Balboa and Apollo Creed. Others line up to take sides with the opposing forces, often surprisingly, and their presence can dramatically change the balance of power. There is a nice illustration of this in *Viva Zapata*, one of my favourite films, when the rebel Zapata (played by Marlon Brando) is captured by the Mexican soldiers who ride away with him, tied to his horse. It is a long journey over rough terrain: the column proceeds at walking pace. Suddenly, from nowhere, a paeon walks alongside them, then another, then another. At first, they are ignored, but then their growing numbers become apparent. Zapata is their hero and the paeons have come to support him. They say nothing, do nothing, just accompany the troops who, before long, are hopelessly outnumbered. The soldiers may have their guns but each of the paeons carries a razor sharp machete. The protest has been silent, without violence, but still overpowering. Zapata is released and has grown in stature, during the course of that ride, from a voice of protest to a leader and folk hero.

It is the nature of the conflict which will decide how each and every character reacts to it. Every decision will be based upon that person's own history, the events that have shaped their lives, their being. It is the philosophy of the worm that turns.

The characters in your screenplay are the instruments of your orchestra. Each has a part to play which, taken in isolation, may be meaningless but, in sum with the others, provides the glorious sound of your concerto. This kind of orchestration is essential. There should be no false notes. The actions of every character must be believable. Only then will we, the audience, believe in the resolution you choose, of the conflict inherent in the premise. This means a close and detailed examination of every character in your story, each being tested by analysis to decide whether, taken together, the provide the right mix of ingredients to fulfil the requirements of your premise.

CHARACTER – THE PSYCHOLOGICAL FACTORS

It is the combination of physical attributes and environmental background which produces the individual psychology. Your story will be about motivation in one way or the other and there are no more powerful motivators than the processes of the mind. What was your own family background – single parent, stable, dysfunctional, only child? What bad experiences marked you – were you bullied, abused? Have these left a minor scar or a severe trauma? What were your ambitions, disappointments; your abilities, qualities; what complexes do you have? Are you happy or unhappy? Do you have imagination? Taste? Judgement? It is essential that you have this detailed information about your characters, no two of which are ever the same – for even minute differences in their tri-dimensional make-up will influence different reactions in any given scenario.

As we have seen, outside appearances are not always genuine reflections of the inner person. A pauper may act rich, ashamed of his poverty, as will a confidence trickster, motivated by his fraudulent intentions. A shy person may cover up his shyness by blustering. Bullies, who have often suffered by being bullied themselves, also bluster. We are considering defence mechanisms here. An ignoramus may deliberately act in a superior, sneering kind of way, to cover his own deficiencies. What a person does and says, the way he or she acts, may in fact be a mirror image of their true selves – the exact opposite. It is the honesty, the clarity, the sincerity of the people you portray which will illuminate your story – it is your characters who must truthfully prove your premise.

FINDING YOUR CHARACTERS

Your characters lie within you and all about you. They exist as relatives, friends, acquaintances, people you see in the street, as well as in your imagination. I emphasise that it is *not* a good idea to copy characters that you have admired in the various films you have seen. They may be admirable in many ways but they were constructed to fulfil a particular purpose, to prove the premise of that film, not any other. Attempt to utilise them and you will be playing false notes again. If you argue that your premise is the same as the film which you saw, then it is all the more important that you create *your* characters to prove *your own* premise. Otherwise you may find yourself charged with plagiarism. Every author is sensitive on this subject, beginners particularly so. That is why it is important for you to establish copyright. But do not think that every idea that comes into your head is in some way exclusive to you: you will find quickly that it is not.

Characters found on the screen, in the theatre, or in the pages of a book, may inspire you, but yours must be your creations and those of no one else. They can look the same, think the same, act the same, but they must have within them that spark of individuality which you, and only you, have ignited within them. That is what will distinguish them from others and the way to do that is to invest them with your thoughts, your opinions, your philosophy, your prejudices. I believe that all writers are frustrated actors, not that many take up the work – they are not sufficiently committed. Besides, the writer wants to play *all* the roles, male and female, hero and villain – every part, not just the lead.

Writing is an exercise in imagination. You should be able to close your eyes and visualise the scene, recognise the people in it, hear every intonation of their voices. You have a cast of thousands from which to choose: look around you. Observe your fellow beings, the way they walk and talk, and try to work out why they do and say things the way they do. Watch closely for the details: the nervous gesture, the pulse in the neck, the furtive look away, the occasional strange grimace. You will find that every character is different; that people you once lumped together as being the same have very different physical, social and psychological traits. And it is not just your view of the characters that is important, it is the way they see themselves. If you think about it, the self-concept defines the outward appearance, the *attitude*. The role is an adopted one: the inner person may be someone quite different. Some actors have a *persona* which they carry from film to film. Think John Wayne, Gary Cooper, Cary Grant, Arnold Schwarzenegger, Clint Eastwood, Harrison Ford, Hugh Grant. Which is not to say they may not be fine actors, capable of playing entirely different roles. Remember Eastwood in *Unforgiven*? *The Bridges of Madison County*?

We listed some of the exterior/interior traits earlier but do not pick and mix from lists to make up a character you think is interesting. Ask yourself why they do what they do, and what is their motivation. Every act, no matter how small, has a purpose, a premise, and that premise must be motivated by the inner being. There is a moral dimension as well: people have *values*. Even the cynical Rick, in *Casablanca*, has a value system. Even more surprisingly, so does the French Captain of Gendarmes played by Claude Raines – he would not admit it but he is a patriot.

A writer needs compassion to realise character; to know is to understand and to understand is to forgive. Even the most dyed-in-the-wool villain's actions are motivated by his background, which may be most cruel. This does not give him license but it may explain his cruelties. You cannot – you would not want to – suffer each and every experience there is but you can observe, analyse, try to comprehend. It is your understanding, the depth of your compassion, which will give perspective to your characters and make them tri-dimensional.

MORE ABOUT CONFLICT

Drama existed long before the written word, or the spoken one come to that. When men were still grunting cave-dwellers, they knew all about drama – it was the struggle to exist. It was the life and death combat with wild animals or fellow hominids. Whether for the competitor or the onlooker, the issue was in doubt: there would only be one winner. The penalty for losing was extinction.

Every day of our lives we face conflict. Without it, we would wither and die. Primitive man had to kill to stay alive. The jungle now is paved with concrete but the instinct for survival remains with us: it is man's strongest motivator. Even in more civilised times, in ancient Greece, there was drama outside the theatre, usually in the guise of sporting events, ritualised contests, wrestling each other for the same goal, the glory of winning. Who would win and who would lose? The audience placed their money and watched with baited breath.

Conflict and the struggle for survival are our principal interests. Our imagination is keenly roused by disastrous floods, earthquakes, mass murders, riots and revolutions. Nothing is more entertaining on television than the destruction caused by the impressive technology of modern wars, preferably being fought by someone else.

The Romans were amazing impressarios. They mounted spectacles which had chariot races, gladiators fighting until death ended the contest, Christians versus lions. The audience even had the power of life and death, with their votes. They liked their conflict and they liked their drama. Just as we did, watching the film.

The Colosseum of today is a giant stadium. Two sets of champions, roared on by their supporting tribes, clash in battle on the green turf. England plays Pakistan, or Australia, at cricket. National pride is at stake. Asked whether he really thought football was a matter of life and death, Bill Shankley, the manager of Liverpool, replied it was more important than that.

Two men meet for the heavyweight championship of the world. The prize money, for the reigning champ, is more than $100 million. We say 'may the best man win' but secretly it is the underdog we want to triumph. Goliath versus Goliath is a good contest but has none of the dramatic impact that David creates in beating the big man. No one ever knows for sure the outcome in any conflict and therein lies the drama. The world champion has lost his crown on more than one occasion as the result of a sucker punch, thrown in desperation. Certain winners on the racecourse have a dismal record.

These are just sporting events, though worthy enough as the subject for great films: *Rocky, Gladiator, Raging Bull*, to name but a few. There is a new dimension given to the story when it impacts directly upon our own lives, when parallels can be drawn, when we want the good little guy – as most of us see ourselves – to win the unequal match against the big, bad guy.

On a scaled-down level we like to observe political squabbles, elections and such like, domestic upheavals, murder trials, demonstrations in the streets. Conflict is all around us, in the most humdrum of daily lives. And in what appear to be the most humdrum people, secret conflicts rage.

Conflict, like change, can be both internal and external. Each and every character will have their own internal conflicts and these will contribute significantly to the outcome of the story, which progresses only through the motivations of the characters. They are not, as a rule, the focus of the story, although they can be, as when the premise is based upon a personal fight against an addiction, like *The Lost Weekend* or *A Hatful of Rain*, or an internal psychological struggle like *Prince of Tides*.

Conflict exists in our everyday life. It does not always have to be fierce or daunting. Ordinary marital squabbles can be a form of conflict, as can the difference between the classes, in a film like *Driving Miss Daisy*, for example, or *Terms of Endearment*, where the differences are interpersonal.

There is the remorseless struggle for existence against the elements, in films like *Volcano* or *Twister*, sometimes clearly focused on the individual, as in Tom Hanks' *Cast Away* (a performance worthy of an Oscar although he did not get one). These are situational films and, as well as drama, can equally be the basis for a comedy.

You cannot write a screenplay without first defining the conflict which will be contained within your story.

THE LOGIC OF SCREENWRITING

The process of change is also repeated in the language: the Greeks called it *dialectics* or *dialogue*. Socrates perfected the art. He stated a proposition to test its truth, which he did by finding a contradiction and then testing that. He arrived at a conclusion – a compromise, a combination of the two, which itself was open to contradiction – contradiction is change.

There are three stages: the thesis – the proposition, the premise – is countered by the antithesis – the argument against – and the resolution of this conflict, the compromise, is another proposition, the synthesis. These three steps comprise the law of all movement. All things change towards their opposite. The present becomes the past; the future, the present. To quote Hegel: 'It is only because a thing contains a contradiction within itself that it moves and acquires impulse and activity.'

Constant change is the essence of all existence. Even stone changes. After centuries of exposure to the elements, it crumbles. Change is an immutable law of nature. Did you ever experiment with iron filings in a physics lesson at school? Their movement was inspired by magnetic polarity, the principle of which can be seen to work in human beings. Characters move from one pole to another, not abruptly but through a series of changes, some of which may be subtle, almost infinitesimal; others which may be rude or even traumatic. Drama is about characters in conflict, characters who will change as a result of that conflict.

If they do not, if they remain constant, then it is bad writing – what is there on the screen for us to watch? We might as well be in an art gallery. Some claim constancy. 'For I am constant as the Northern Star,' says Julius Caesar, explaining why he would not grant pardon to a miscreant, a friend of Cassius. It was a bad move. Caesar was not motionless, he had ambition, too much of it for Cassius wanted him cut down to size. How could he do that? Only by whispering flattering words into the ear of Brutus, Caesar's trusted friend, the only Roman of equal stature. Brutus loved Caesar: he said so. But he loved Rome more, and Cassius played on that. Brutus, an honourable man ('So are they all, all honourable men,' as Mark Antony says) commits an act of dishonour. Caesar, the Colossus who bestrode Rome, was felled, the victim of his own ambition.

DIALOGUE

Dialogue is a fascinating device. It is a device: it is most unlikely that your characters will speak like their real-life counterparts. You would not want them to do that. People stammer, tell stories with convoluted logic, sprinkle the conversation with *non-sequiturs*. What we require is something that may not be truthful, in the sense that it is not entirely accurate, but which does effectively perform the functions required of it: to drive the story and to illuminate character.

There is of course an inner truth, the integrity of our premise, our purpose in writing the screenplay, and it is to help achieve this aim that we need dialogue. But it is only a tool: dialogue is deceptive.

Read or listen to Pinter. It sounds like tape-recorder stuff. All the hesitance is there, the ineloquent pauses, the sentences that peter out pointlessly. But now go out with a tape-recorder yourself and see if you can snatch similar dialogue from similar people, and then compare them. You will see a marked difference. Transcribe what you have and then tell me it is dialogue. It is not. Listen to Pinter again. It may *sound* real but it is not. It is a distillation, an essence: it conveys very precisely that which the author wishes to convey. It *sounds* right because the writer has observed, listened, and then reproduced the rhythms, the *speech patterns* that suggest authenticity. The *selection* is brilliant: the only elements used are those that define character or push forward the story. It may *sound* static: it is anything but – indeed it is dynamic. Paradoxical though it may be, every *non-sequitur* has a purpose.

Take another master of what sounds like *real* dialogue, Mike Leigh. Leigh constructs his plays and films almost entirely on observation. He works with an *ensemble*, a cast that understand his methods, many of whom have worked with him before. He will spend months rehearsing a piece, a length of preparation that is quite rare in the theatre and almost totally unknown in the world of movie-making. Each actor has to create his or her own character, following the outlines described by the director. It is an extraordinary achievement. The actors develop their own characters and in so doing, in effect write the film – the dialogue at least. But the words, whatever they may be, must still convey the purpose of the author, to prove the premise he has selected. And that is *all* they are required to do– anything extraneous is removed. In this method of work, in a manner of speaking, the editing precedes the film. The result is joyful. He derives eloquence and truth from stumbling phrases and repeated clichés. Mike Leigh is a towering talent who can truly be described as the *auteur* of his films.

I knew Mike Leigh's work in the theatre, of course, but could hardly believe it when he told me that, while preparing *Topsy Turvy*, he employed the same techniques in filming: I could not imagine anyone meeting the cost of employing actors over such a long period. But then most actors would give their right hands to work with him and I suppose winning a few prizes at Cannes does allow a certain license.

You might ask whether dialogue is of prime importance, since it is the medium of film for which we are writing. Certainly, picture is important and, if you see what is happening, it is usually redundant to report it. It is always a good idea to keep the dialogue as spare as possible and seeing is believing, while words can lie. Which is not to say that images cannot lie but that would have to be contrived, the way Hitchcock used to put objects in the forefront of a shot which would gain our attention for no purpose at all, other than to take our eye off where the ball really was – the McGuffin.

I read somewhere that 85 per cent of everything we learn, we learn visually: I do not know how true it is but it is a statistic worth keeping in mind. In everyday life, however, talking is our major means of communication and so, naturally, we expect to see those patterns repeated on the screen. The experience is a 'screened' one though: I have already indicated that a feeling of authenticity can be conveyed by the repetition of rhythms and speech patterns. The way people speak is all important because it gives us a clear indication of who they are and where they come from: we need to know that because everything that is going to happen – the *action* of the picture – is going to spring from their characters.

I used to teach English once, in the Army, and my party piece was a kind of imitation of Professor Higgins, going round a new class and identifying – usually correctly – where each and every one had come from. But accents are easy and can be misleading. It is not just the geography but the principal influences in people's lives that will determine the way they speak. In early years, it is their parentage but, as soon as they go to school, it is their peers.

There used to be a kind of standard or BBC intonation employed by most of the educated classes: now it is more likely to be Estuary English. Even so, it is not just the accent but the grammar, the phrasing, the range of vocabulary, even the choice of subject which can inform you pretty well of that person's background. It is important that your characters be accurately drawn, that we are convinced of their authenticity, so that we believe they have the courage, skill or ability to play their part in forwarding the action of the screenplay – or the ignorance and stupidity. Negative characters can be as important as positive ones. It is worth repeating that, in essence, dialogue has two functions: to move the story forward and to reveal character.

There is another element to remember, though not necessarily a function, and that is that dialogue often entertains. The primary purpose of most of the dialogue in a Groucho Marx picture is to make us laugh. The plot is simple enough not to need a lot of explanation and Groucho wears a character like he might a suit of clothes: we look at him, whatever the cut may be. Mae West relied on her one-liners, as did Jack Benny. Each of them carries their own *persona* like a piece of baggage.

There have been many excellent films made from the plays of Oscar Wilde. The premises are usually quite simple, no matter how convoluted the plot. You go to see Oscar Wilde for the sparkling wit and you would most likely go, for the same reason, to see a Noel Coward play. This is not to say that they do not fulfil the rules of dramatic writing: they do. But the *emphasis* of the dialogue is on its cleverness: it is difficult for us to believe that such finely honed wit could be natural speech. So we do not believe in the characters: we feel we are watching a puppet show. It is vastly entertaining but it diminishes the *purpose* of the piece, if there ever was one other than to entertain us. It is a kind of conjuring trick where it is not only the quickness of the hand, but also our concentration on the patter, that deceives the eye.

Films can have a serious purpose but be funny as well. I cannot recall a more hilarious film than *Tootsie*, where Dustin Hoffman as the frustrated actor discovers, through female impersonation, the exploitation of women. *As Good As It Gets* is a serious love story and an examination of male prejudices. Probably only Jack Nicholson could pull off the task of making us believe that Helen Hunt, for all her poverty, would put up with his rudeness and grumpiness.

An interesting example of *purposeful* comedy writing can be seen in the long-running television sitcom *Frasier*. The dialogue is scintillating but always believable. After all, these two brothers consider wit and sophistication to be the highest of aims: they probably practise their one-liners in the privacy of their bedrooms. They play off against Marty, the dad, Roz and Daphne, all of whom are sharp and streetwise – and are there to puncture their pomposity. The Crane brothers are a brilliant concoction: some of their smartest observations must be way ahead of the audience's comprehension but it does not matter: what matters is that they are obviously preening in their usual insufferable style – and will be quickly brought to ground. The conflict is always there: the embarrassment of the brothers at being so much better educated, so much more sophisticated, than their ex-cop dad for whom Frasier, nevertheless, feels he has to provide a home. Their inner turmoil, which they recognise, being psychiatrists themselves, but will not admit, is that socially they are ashamed of their father – a situation which probably hits home with many of their viewers, as must Marty's wry amusement at his stuck-up, over-educated kids – where did he go wrong?

If the conflict is present in the nature of the characters and the situation they find themselves in, then the dialogue will propel the story forward almost without assistance. Since the conflict, and the eventual premise, spring from the characters themselves, then every speech must be reflective of the three dimensions we have already identified. Be wary of too much dialogue. There used to be a kind of film characterised as 'European', which usually meant a long voice-over narrative, often, though intermittent, from start to finish. It also meant long, introspective speeches from the actors spelling out the nature of their own characters – a background we should be aware of from their physical presence, the way they walk and talk. It also often meant long soliloquies. Soliloquies have their place in the theatre – Hamlet is a master of the device – but very rarely on film. Thank heavens that these days when an American talks about a 'European' film, he most likely means something like *The Full Monty*.

'THE BRITISH ARE COMING!' (BUT WHEN?)

When an English writer, Colin Welland (better known to some as the actor from *Kes*), won an Oscar for an original screenplay, it was – or we hoped it was – some kind of turning point for British films. 'The British are coming!' he yelled from the rostrum. The producer of *Chariots of Fire*, David (now Lord) Puttnam, returned from the ceremony to attend the Annual Conference of the Association of Cinematograph, Television and Allied Technicians. Centre-stage on the platform, he held the Oscar aloft. How we all cheered.

The 1980s also brought *Rocky* in successive versions, Eddie Murphy and Arnold Schwarzenegger. The fees demanded, and commanded, by leading actors went through the roof and have continued their passage skyward ever since: a film often costs only a fraction of its budget; it is the talent which absorbs the bulk of the funding. It irritates me when producers complain about the cost of technicians when stars take by far the lion's share and distribution costs as much as the picture did to make.

After *Chariots of Fire* came *Gandhi*, taking another hatful of Oscars. The British successes worldwide inspired Columbia Pictures to invite

David Puttnam to become the studio head. His stay there was brief, however. He sought to curb the financial excesses and his proposals were far too sensible and straightforward for the dream factory: the stars, the big agents, the major independent producers – the people who ran Hollywood– all ganged up on him.

They probably could not stand the idea of a Brit telling them what to do. When he left it was Hollywood's loss, even if a few sharks gained. David is an honest, conscientious man (a description that brings shudders out there) and, having had a successful career as a producer, he now seeks to give something back to the business. We often meet at various functions. He is our senior statesman (after Richard Attenborough) and takes a great interest in the training of those young technicians who will be the core of a successful British – even European – industry.

Here are two films from the 1980s which, in a way, typify the differences between indigenous production in the USA and the UK. These differences are mostly about scale.

RAGING BULL (1980)

Raging Bull picked up a host of nominations and won two Oscars, for De Niro and Thelma Schoonmaker (the brilliant editor). An exciting, raw and brutal film, it confirmed the oustanding talents of the director, Martin Scorsese.

It is the story of Jake La Motta, who was once the middleweight boxing champion of the world. A legend in fight circles, he finished up an overweight has-been, trading on his name, entertaining in clubs. This is *Rocky* for real – the scenes in the ring are outstanding. We almost feel the punches, we certainly wince at them. We duck the spray from the fighters' sweaty bodies. We turn our heads away at the gristle and gore as the blows smash home.

It has the theme of the little man again, the slum kid who batters his way out of the Bronx. His gift for violence, however, has the opposite effect on his private life. Indomitable in the ring, his inner doubts force him into fierce jealousies. He loves his wife but has no idea how to treat her. De Niro's performance as the courageous, bewildered, frustrated La Motta has become the stuff of legend itself. At least he was rewarded. No one will ever know how Scorsese missed out on the best director award that year.

GREGORY'S GIRL (1980)

Nothing could provide a greater antithesis to *Raging Bull* and yet in its own small way, this is just as fine a film. Its budget would hardly have met that for De Niro's personal entourage but it was still hugely successful, perhaps because it was so different. Jake La Motta may have been a great fighter but he was not the most pleasant of human beings. The shy and gawky Gregory, played by John Gordon Sinclair, could not be more likeable, as indeed were the rest of the cast – what a nice change to see teenagers portrayed as ordinary, good-natured kids and not as thick, sex-mad junkies.

This film by Bill Forsyth (another true *auteur*) was modestly intended as a television movie but stakes its place emphatically on the big screen. When a girl (Dee Hepburn) wins a place in the hitherto exclusively male football team, it is at the expense of Gregory, who promptly falls in love with her. This is not a feminist tract but a film about the growing pains of adolescence. It is witty, touching and affectionate and gives you a warm glow when you come out of the cinema. How inspiring it is to see an optimistic film, one that believes in the innate decency of human nature but is not cloyingly sentimental, as perhaps a Frank Capra attempt at the same story might have been.

This is all that is best about British cinema. We do make these little gems. We can also make big ones but we only do it for the Americans. When are British investors going to believe in our indigenous film-making potential?

THE TURNING POINT

Does every story have to have a beginning, a middle and an end? Yes, but not necessarily in that order. Many fine films have started with the end and have then gone on to reveal how the character reached it, like *American Beauty*. Another example was the *film noir* classic *Double Indemnity* with Fred MacMurray, unusually playing a straight role, and Barbara Stanwyck, who was nominated as best actress for her performance. A Billy Wilder/Raymond Chandler team effort – it makes the mouth water, does it not? – Fred MacMurray tells the story in flashback. Flashback is another device that needs to be handled with great care. Generally speaking, we believe that what we see in flashback is what has happened, but it can of course be just a person's point of view – and mistaken at that, viz. the ambivalent example in *Rules of Engagement* and a straightforward cheat in Hitchock's *Stage Fright*, starring Marlene Dietrich. What the end must have is satisfaction and, preceding it, from the start, anticipation.

What is the turning point in *American Beauty*? Is it when he meets the young nymphette and he realises how boring his life is, how sterile his marriage? Of course it is. What is the turning point for Holly Martins in *The Third Man*? It is when Holly discovers that his friend has died in an accident – for which no one has a convincing explanation. The ingredients of his character, curiosity and stubbornness, carry the story forward thereafter. Think of any films you have seen recently, or know well. Ask yourself what the premise is and who is the protagonist? What was the event that pushed the protagonist into following the course of events he or she does, to prove the premise? That is the turning point.

It is sometimes called *the point of attack*, which means the same thing. It is when the life of the protagonist is inexorably changed as the result of an outside event which, initially anyway, he can do nothing about. Then something *does* spur him into action – he is provoked, like Holly Martins. But what is it that makes some characters start a chain of events which could well destroy them? People like Erin Brockovich?

The answer is necessity. Come the hour, come the man – or woman. There must be an external or internal *need* for characters like that to act the way they do. Which means there must be something at stake – and not something trivial. What gives your screenplay weight and substance is the importance of your premise. Remember it is the *premise* that is important, not the subject. It is the *principle* that matters.

The event itself must be a *crisis* for someone. For Helen Hunt's character in *As Good As It Gets*, it was the inability of the doctors to give relief to her sick son. Going off on a tangent, that inability was simply because she could not pay their bills. For me, that weakened the impact and, Oscar-winner or not, made it a less-than-great film. As someone brought up with the National Health Service, the injustice for me was that a sick child could be ignored because his mother was broke. The fairy story bit where grumpy old Jack Nicholson sent his own doctor round, with money no object in assisting the boy's recovery, cut no ice with me. There was a blatant injustice, a foetid morality, that no one in the film challenged. I guess that is the American way of life.

Someone stood up against corporate greed and the power of the mighty dollar: Erin Brockovich. She was broke and unemployed and a single mother – that was the crisis in her life. It was not fair, and she rebelled against the injustice. Erin Brockovich is a great heroine, an example to us all. As is the film, being a model of construction – well almost. The only thing that grates is that after a titanic struggle – not between Titans but David and Goliath – the chemicals company caves in: they do not go out of business, it just costs them a lot of money; much, much more than they had ever expected to pay. What does that prove?

Every crisis will lead to a climax which must be somehow resolved. Get these words fixed firmly in your head. You will find that as you progress your story, as you outline the chain of events, each one of them – each complete scene – will contain the same ingredients. Almost inevitably, your story will start low-key: you must have some-where to go. As you move constantly from crisis to climax to resolution

– which ignites yet another crisis – you achieve a dynamic in your storytelling, an exposition of rising conflict which will keep your audience glued to its seats.

Let us recap again so that you can see how all the elements of construction weld themselves together:

- You physically begin your screenplay with a *crisis*, one which will allow you to prove your *premise*.
- That crisis is a *turning point* in someone's life. It is a moment of *decision* for your *protagonist*.
- That *decision* will be to stand up against the *antagonist*, who at first will be vastly superior in strength.
- It is at that moment, the *turning point*, that the *decision* sparks off the *conflict*.
- It is in *conflict* that your *characters* will be exposed, showing their true mettle. Those characters will be *orchestrated*, to ensure that each and every one plays their part – whether they are on one side or the other – in eventually proving the *premise*.
- The characters will be exposed through their *dialogue*, which will also drive the story forward. *Conflict* comes from the clash of *characters*, who reveal themselves in their *dialogue*.

'AND NOW THE END IS NEAR'

The 1990s saw some good films made, along with a fair amount of dross. Quentin Tarantino proved that *Reservoir Dogs* was no fluke, making the remarkable *Pulp Fiction*, while *Four Weddings and a Funeral* established a new kind of 'British' film, a formula successfully followed up by *Notting Hill* and *Bridget Jones's Diary*. A surprise hit was the modest but thumpingly successful comedy, *The Full Monty*, and *The English Patient* collected a hatful of Oscars.

From outside these shores, another unpretentious film which became a worldwide hit was *Shine*, from Australia, while perhaps the most innovative films of the decade were those composing the *Three Colours* trilogy, individually *Red*, *White* and *Blue*, from the marvellous Kzrysztof Kieslowski.

The end of the decade produced the big one however; not a spectacularly good film but a good spectacular one – with *Titanic* breaking all budgets hitherto known and breaking all box-office records too, reputedly taking in more than a billion dollars.

For me, the outstanding screenplays of that period were of the films discussed below.

THREE COLOURS: RED (1994)

This was the richest of the *Three Colours* trilogy, named in honour of the French flag and the revolutionary ideals it represents; liberty, equality, fraternity. Although the three films stand alone, and are almost equally enjoyable, this was the last, and in the final sequence all the themes are tied together, bringing back some of the characters from the earlier films.

The story is a remarkable one, intriguing but with seemingly disconnected incidents, which eventually makes total sense and makes us feel we have learned something, enriched our own lives by the experience of seeing this film. Jean-Louis Trintignant plays the part of the lonely judge who finds companionship by tapping into other folks' telephone conversations. Irene Jacob is the beautiful model who accidentally runs over his dog and then takes it to his home. The theme of fraternity is expressed in the relationship which grows up between them. They are an odd couple but that it necessary in order to prove the premise, that we are all dependent on each other.

It should have won the Oscar for best screenplay in 1994 but Hollywood likes to honour its own, even if in this case it was a young upstart called Quentin Tarantino for his smash-hit *Pulp Fiction*.

PULP FICTION (1994)

This was the second-best screenplay of that year in my opinion but it was a great movie, maybe deserving of the best film award, certainly more than the thoroughly likeable but inferior *Forrest Gump*, which did take that honour. However, Tarantino did nothing less than re-invent the modern thriller: no mean achievement.

It was good because it was fresh, daring and innovative. The premise was probably in the title, the suggestion that life in the end is much like pulp fiction, and so it must be if one enters the dark world that Tarantino characters inhabit. It is these characters, beyond the ken of most of us but still somehow totally credible, which make the picture so believable and compelling to watch.

The story – the three stories – are related in an amazing way, like pieces in a jigsaw puzzle, and we can only comprehend the whole when we see the beginning, at the end – if you follow me. The stories brush up against each other, sometimes almost accidentally, while having a life and purpose of their own.

It is a film that has scenes which linger in the memory: the idle chatter of the two hit-men en route to their victim; Uma Thurman overdosing on heroin; Harvey Keitel as a cleaner-up of dead bodies; and a tough gang boss meeting his nemesis in the shape of two freaks who rape him. The approach has the verve and attack of someone determined to be noticed – and he was.

SUB-TEXT

Sometimes, what we do not say is a lot more meaningful than that which we do. Harold Pinter conveys so much more in his pauses than he does in direct dialogue. We are not writing for the radio but for the screen and people's gestures can often be more informative than their halting, stumbling words. A raised eyebrow or a shrug can be extremely eloquent. We can even say one thing and mean the exact opposite, like the wife in *American Beauty*, like Mark Antony in *Julius Caesar*.

Dialogue is not a single-dimensional entity. If it were, it would just convey information from one source to another and that would be the end of it. But dialogue is far more subtle, far more flexible. The text contains flat statements. Just the intonations of voice can slant the meaning considerably. The words are driven by the thoughts but if the desire is *not* to pass on information, the words will not reflect the thoughts. They will convey what you want the other person to *think* you are thinking but, again, they too are aware of sub-text. This is dictated by the inner being. Desires can be suppressed, information withheld. A psychiatrist looks for the sub-text of what you are saying. It is what you really mean, or intend – though you may not know it yourself.

The opposite of sub-text is overtness. Dialogue can be over-stated or blatant. Describing in dialogue what you can already see in picture is redundancy, unless its purpose is to point out, for example, that the image is misleading. Pictures can have a sub-text too.

Redundant, glaringly obvious statements are often called *on the nose* dialogue. We do not tell stories in a simple alphabetical manner, proceeding from A to Z. We dodge around, we are diverted: you would not believe a story told so directly. If all characters said what they meant, that would be a shocking example of on the nose dialogue. Where is the richness and diversity of spirit that divides each of us from the other? When people say exactly what someone of that class and background, that physical presence, would be expected to say, we call them stereotypes. The blatant dialogue of stereotypes has no sub-text.

Drama has conflict and conflict has consequences, often damaging. If you find someone in an alleyway lying shattered and bleeding, you do not say to them: 'Are you all right?' It is overt, it is *on the nose*, it is a hackneyed phrase used more by way of reaction – clearly the unfortunate being is *not* all right.

Another form of sub-text is that which may be derived from playing the same dialogue but in a different or unusual setting. The sub-text conveyed to us by a man and a woman chatting in a car might be quite different from what it will be when we discover they are Bonnie and Clyde. It is a common device in television writing, where a good deal of expository dialogue is required, to break the usual pattern by giving it unexpected patterns – the spy feeding the birds in the park has become a visual cliché. There are sometimes desperate efforts at variation, often ridiculous. How many times have you seen boardroom dialogue delivered by contestants at archery, or squash? Good writing does not need these gimmicks for there will be no on the nose dialogue (or action) to cover up: there will be a clarifying sub-text which still has subtlety.

A MODERN SCREENPLAY

Let us take a look at a modern screenplay that is beautifully crafted and which demonstrates many of the points we have been considering. Its writer is American but the film's director was British. Interestingly, both of them came from theatrical backgrounds, on either side of the ocean.

Indeed, *American Beauty* was first conceived as a stage play and, note this, it was Alan Ball's first produced feature screenplay. So it is possible to get a break, and to make it big from the start and, if you think that was a fluke, the same thing happened to Sam Mendes for, although an acclaimed director in the theatre, this was his feature film directorial debut. So there are people out there looking for new talent and, in this case, the gamble of producers Dan Jinks and Bruce Cohen certainly paid off in gold.

The premise of the film is 'Life is worth living' and the only way to show that is to begin with someone whose life is hell and transform his character to prove the premise. First, there is a brief teaser (a flashback from a later scene) in which the 16-year-old Jane Burnham complains about her father to an unseen boyfriend, who offers to kill him for her. And so we have suspect number one in an intriguing murder story for we discover immediately, from the voice-over narration of Lester Burnham, her father, that in less than a year he will be dead. So this is not a whodunit but a whoisgoingtodoit. There will be no shortage of suspects. And the device of using a dead narrator allows the author to establish immediately that this was a middle-aged man in crisis, in an unhappy marriage and remote from his daughter.

Every incident in this scenario has a purpose, even though we do not perceive it at the time. Why the emphasis on their having gay neighbours, for example? Surely homosexuality cannot be part of the plot? It is, but not in the way you may think.

And then there is Carolyn, the wife, a real estate agent, whose impatience and dissatisfaction with her husband is openly expressed, even if couched in sardonic politeness: 'Lester, could you make me a little later, please? Because I'm not quite late enough.' A little heavy on the sub-text.

As if Lester's life at home were not hell enough, he has worked in a job he despises for fourteen years and, if he does not humbly toe the line, is about to get the sack. At dinner that night he tries to explain his predicament to his wife and child, neither of whom show any sympathy for him. He is a man alone with his unhappiness.

We see a series of apparently disconnected events, all of them in fact meticulously pre-plotted in the cause of rising conflict. Carolyn is an obsessive but unsuccessful saleswoman, who is deeply jealous of the leading realtor in the area, Buddy Kane. She is tense, uncertain, on the edge of a nervous breakdown, all of which she conceals beneath a brightly confident veneer. Ball gets all this neatly in just one scene, showing one sales pitch with four different clients, each in different rooms, all of whom pass on buying. The scenarist is a master of economy.

A part of this story is about children and parents and the gulf between them, but thankfully this is written without the usual guilt and sentiment that often jar in American films. Jane is open enough in her dislike of her warring parents and they know it. Indeed, as Lester tells Carolyn: 'She hates me ... and she hates you.' They go through the motions of being good parents, even forcing themselves to see Jane in a show at school, performed by the Dancing Spartanettes.

We watch the pain of the hapless Lester and though we know the worm will always turn, when will he, and how? What will be the turning point in his life, in the story? And then we see Angela, Jane's friend, and we know. She is the nymphette supreme, blonde, beautiful and sexy with parted lips that are an open invitation. Lester is smitten. All thoughts of his wife, his job, the other parents disappear as he fantasises in a world of his own – but with Angela.

They do meet, afterwards in the car park. The writer effortlessly captures the boredom and embarrassment of youth, in the presence of their parents. And their astuteness. The sexually provocative Angela is immediately aware of Lester's interest: she has seen it in middle-aged men many times. She opines that Jane's mother and father don't have sex any more, and she is right. Lester finds his sexual relief in masturbation, and admits it.

We have a turning point. Lester is in love with a sixteen-year-old who is his daughter's best friend. A crisis, indeed. What does the young lady think about it? As we find, from a dialogue with Jane, she is nonchalantly aware of Lester's interest. Angela wants to be a model – she wants anything except to be ordinary. And we get the impression she will sleep with anyone, do anything, that gets her where she wants to be. From the dialogue, we learn she is already sexually promiscuous, though Jane is a virgin.

Back at home, ex-Marine Colonel Fitts has arrived to take up residence in the empty house next door. He has a depressed wife and a very strange teenage son, Ricky, who likes to video everything including the neighbours, day or night. The two gay men (both called Jim) who live on the other side of the Burnhams' house, arrive on the doorstep with flowers, to greet the family to the neighbourhood. Jim introduces the other Jim as his partner. The confused Colonel thinks he means business partner. It is quite a while before the penny drops.

The Colonel rages to his son about these faggots. Ricky is obviously an easy-going guy but has to go along with what his father says: we get the impression he would be in physical danger if he did not. We also learn that Ricky is earning some fairly substantial sums, though his father is unaware of it. We discover how later, at a ballroom function, where Ricky is waiting tables and Lester and Carolyn are also present. She introduces him to the king of the real estate agents, Buddy Kane. Lester embarrasses her, as always: he is already getting drunk fast. Ricky introduces himself to Lester as the new neighbour and, outside, offers to sell him marijuana. He confesses he only does these gigs as a cover for his other activities. When Ricky's boss threatens to sack him, the boy coolly quits the job, earning Lester's admiration. Meanwhile, Carolyn is flirting with Buddy Kane, the business rival she so envies.

Jane is at home, with Angela, when they arrive back. Angela flutters her eyelashes at Lester who immediately plunges into another sexual fantasy about her. Staying over, she teases Jane as well, saying she quite fancies Lester and that he would have a great body if he worked out, a conversation overheard by Lester, listening at the door. Jane and Angela catch Ricky trying to video-tape them. Angela knows Ricky from sometime back: she says he is a weirdo who spent time in a mental hospital. Once again, Ball is carefully pre-plotting. The pieces of the jigsaw are being put in place.

Ricky has this curious obsession with video-taping everything that goes on, even Lester clearing out his garage so that he can make a gym in there, somewhere to work out. Ricky has a room full of expensive hi-fi and video gear and a desk where he keeps his stash of marijuana in a false-bottomed drawer. We wonder how he gets away with it, with such a strict father, especially when the Colonel comes round on an inspection, demanding a urine sample from his son to test for drugs. But this is routine for Ricky who already has a system to combat these enquiries, keeping a clean sample always on hand, drawn from someone else.

Lester has taken up jogging along with the two Jims, to get himself fit. They are watched with a beady eye by the Colonel as they return, when Lester goes into his garage to do some weight-lifting. Colonel Fitts is beginning to have grave doubts about Lester, especially since he seems to have struck up a friendship with Ricky.

Under the influence of pot, and madly in love, Lester is a new man. He has changed. No longer prepared to be browbeaten at work, his insolence earns him the sack at last. Lester is only concerned with getting a decent pay-off which, since he knows where the skeletons are hidden, he achieves. Head held high, he walks away. Life has suddenly become an adventure again.

At the school, Ricky is still photographing Jane. She asks him to stop but we sense a growing empathy between them. The shallow Angela insists Ricky is mentally unstable. Maybe he is. There is an aura of unhappiness about him. We get the feeling there is a tragedy brewing. Ball is carefully plotting again. We can guess who will be the centre of the tragedy. We already know Lester is going to die. But how? And if violently, by whose hand?

Carolyn is in a motel with Buddy Kane. She still wants sex, as does her husband, but not with each other. Ball plots carefully ahead again. Buddy admits to a passion for guns – will he end Lester's life? Carolyn wants to go on the shooting range with him. Will she?

Ricky and Jane are slowly getting on, walking home together now from school. She questions him about his obsession with filming. He explains that through the camera lens, he sees beauty in everything. He is clearly very unhappy at home. He introduces Jane to his tyranised mother, then shows Jane the Colonel's collection of guns and Nazi memorabilia. Guns again – Ricky has access and so does the Colonel.

At dinner, Carolyn does her best to humiliate Lester in front of Jane, because he has lost his job. She does not know he has applied for another, as a short order clerk in a fast food eaterie – that would kill her. Ball is plotting carefully again. He does not want her to know – yet. Lester explodes with rage: he just is not taking this shit from his wife any more. Jane finds the behaviour of both her parents totally gross. She tells her mother so and Carolyn slaps her. Jane goes to her room and sees Ricky filming her. Standing in the window, she begins to take off her clothes. Ricky keeps filming. Then the Colonel comes in and catches him. He is furious because he knows Ricky has been rummaging in his study. He knocks the boy about, badly. Jane watches.

Lester is enjoying his new life. He is getting more and more fit, working out, and it shows. He has got rid of his car and bought an old Firebird, satisfying a boyhood dream. He practically lives in the garage now and has built a model jeep. The separation seems complete but Ball still shows us another side – nothing is entirely black and white. Indeed there is a moment when we think the two might kiss and make up – but Carolyn spoils it. She does not mean to, she just cannot help herself. This is great character portrayal. We know that Carolyn's background is such that this moment is inevitable. She is imprisoned in the life she has built for herself. Lester has escaped from his.

Jane and Ricky are lovers now. He tells her something of his past. He too has never been able to escape from his domineering father. He is clearly walking on a line between madness and sanity. Jane complains about her own father, having a crush on her best friend. Ricky asks her coolly whether she wants him to kill Lester and we suddenly realise we are reprising the opening scene of the movie when she replies: 'Would you?' Again, Ricky becomes number one suspect of a killing that has yet to take place. In every scene there is a crisis followed by a climax, and then a conclusion, which becomes a crisis again in the next scene. Note the pre-plotting again. We take Ricky seriously because he has just confirmed that he did have a stay in a mental hospital.

There is an old Hollywood maxim: 'First you tell 'em, and then you show 'em' and Ball uses this to great effect. Lester as narrator tells us that this may be the last day of his life. Ball is turning the screw. Tension. Rising conflict. We begin to see how it might happen. Jane confronts him about the way he looks at Angela – and Angela is staying over that night. The Colonel is watching Lester, of whom he strongly disapproves, but who seems to have a buddy-buddy relationship with his son. He does not know of course that Ricky is supplying Lester with grass. Suspicious, he goes into Ricky's room and plays over some tapes. One of them is of Lester working out – looking just like the two gay men. Colonel Fitts is apparently such a stereotype of the tough marine, we just laugh at his discomfiture but, again, we are being cleverly manipulated by the writer. Alan Ball does not write stereotypes, as we will see.

When Carolyn and Buddy Kane return after an afternoon's love-making, they stop at a drive-through for a hamburger, only to find Lester serving them. Carolyn is mortified and Lester feels finally vindicated. When he gets home, he finds Angela there with Jane. He goes to the garage for a pot-fuelled work-out, only to find he is out of grass. He beeps Ricky next door, who makes an excuse about having to see Jane and goes on over. While all this is going on, Carolyn is being dumped by Buddy Kane. If you count, the writer is telling us seven different stories simultaneously but they all gel so beautifully we are unaware of it.

The Colonel looks across at the garage and he sees Lester counting out a wad of bills, ready to pay for the dope. When Ricky enters, he hands over the dough. The Colonel watches, speechless. Lester has his top off and, from the Colonel's point of view, looks stark naked. The Colonel has long wondered how Ricky seemed to earn so much money and now, as he sees Ricky appearing to go down on Lester (all in the Colonel's mind, of course), he figures it out. It is a very funny scene but pregnant with tragedy, all beautifully pre-plotted.

Lester goes into the house where Angela gently flirts with him but now he meets her glance with challenge: this is the new man. It is Angela's turn to back off. Ricky returns to his home to be directly accused by his father. He starts to protest his innocence but then suddenly sees that this is a way out! If he admits to being a faggot, his father will throw him out of the house! So he does. And so does the Colonel.

He is not too pleased at seeing Ricky return to Lester's house. We see his anger and realise he could kill Lester – is this how it is going to end? But Carolyn, driving home, is also in a highly emotional state, for which she blames her husband. And she has a gun – from the shooting range. Will she be the one?

Up in Jane's room, Ricky is asking her to go to New York with him. Angela is deriding them both and still teasing Jane about seducing Lester. They have a row and Angela flounces out, then sits on the steps, crying. Lester is drying himself off after his work-out when the Colonel appears. The dialogue is an amazing *double entendre*, absolutely truthful but giving the impression that Lester really is a homosexual. The Colonel certainly thinks so. He kisses him. It is a great *coup de théatre*. Lester gently puts him straight and the Colonel runs off. Lester returns to the house to find Angela, who confesses she and Jane have had a fight. To punish Jane, she starts to flirt again. Lester meets this head-on. He kisses her, admits his fantasies, starts to strip her off. Then there is another *coup de théatre*. Angela is no *femme fatale* at all – in fact, she is a virgin. Everything she has boasted about is a lie.

Seeing her child-like vulnerability revealed for the first time, Lester is suddenly solicitous, paternal. He backs off, soothes the confused Angela, makes her a peanut butter sandwich. It is still an intimate picture and Carolyn is at that moment arriving at the house – with her gun. We can see just how this picture is going to end – but we are wrong.

Lester asks Angela about Jane, his daughter. Angela tells him she is going off to New York with Ricky, and that she is happy. And that makes Lester happy. He suddenly feels good about himself. He has almost totally turned his life around. Angela goes to the bathroom. Lester looks at the photograph of himself and Carolyn, and Jane when she was just a child. Happiness stares back at him. For the first time in years, he feels content. Then a gun is pointed at the base of his neck. It fires.

Ricky and Jane run down the stairs to find Lester dead. Lester's voice-over takes up the narration again. The scene is replayed, with this time Jane and Ricky hearing the shot, in her room. Then another flashback in time, just a matter of seconds, as we see Carolyn, walking up to the front door. She hears the shot too. So Carolyn is not the killer.

Then we see Colonel Fitts, entering his study, taking off his blood-stained gloves, returning the pistol to a cabinet. And now we know. But this picture was never about who pulled the trigger, not really. It was about a man finding happiness at last. If only for a few moments before his death, he discovered or rediscovered the beauty of life, knew that life is worth living – too late but without rancour.

Watch the film over and over again, and others I have given especial mention to, like *Erin Brockovich* and *The Third Man*. Analyze them. They are all first-class examples of scenario writing. There are many others, a number of which have been brought to your attention. Judge them against the principles you have learned here, of good writing. Do not copy them but absorb the lessons they have for you. You will learn from every film you see, when you learn how to see. This will not make you a great writer. But it will show you how to write.

SIX QUESTIONS ABOUT YOUR SCREENPLAY

1) Do you have a clear, well thought-out *premise*? Are you *pre-plotting* it?
2) Are there a *protagonist* and an *antagonist* who, in the course of their mutual *conflict*, will prove the premise? Are all your characters *orchestrated* to contribute to that same end?
3) What is the *turning point* in someone's life that will precipitate the conflict?
4) Do your principal characters *change*? Is there pole-to-pole movement? Does the situation *change*? Are the *transitions* effected smoothly, and not jerkily?
5) Does your screenplay have a logical, dialectic basis? Does the story, through its characters, move from *crisis* to *climax* to *resolution* in a pattern of rising conflict?
6) Does your *dialogue* reveal the characters and, in so doing, progress the story? Does it sound *natural*? Is the *sub-text* sufficiently clear for there to be no confusion – except of course when confusion is required?

FORM, LAY-OUT, PRESENTATION

All right, you have made copious notes, you have consulted all the checklists, you are physically ready to write your screenplay. Very roughly speaking (it depends on the proportions of dialogue and description) each page will run just under a minute, so for a 100-minute script you will want to write 120 to 130 pages. These days, computer programs can format your script for you but you might as well know the general rules. These programs are rather like having a chauffeur – that is fine so long as you do not forget how to drive.

The lay-out of the foolscap (or American quarto) page is pretty standard. You will need margins of one inch all round with a wider margin of about an inch and a half (the industry rarely subscribes to metric) on the left-hand side for binding. Numbering of the pages is top right or centre-bottom. Scenes are usually numbered though some hold this is not necessary. I think it is and I will explain why: your script is more than a literary document, it is also a blueprint. Personally, when I submit a script, I expect it to become a production. This is not always the case but if it is I have made life easier for all those people who now have to go through it and break it down according to their individual skills. It will still not of course be a shooting script but these are nonetheless important preliminaries to it becoming one.

When you describe each scene you will head it with the location in capital letters, first indicating whether it is INTERIOR or EXTERIOR and whether the lighting is for DAY or NIGHT. You can then describe the action within the scene. Thus:

1. EXT. PRISON COURTYARD. DAY

TWO MEN are building a gallows. The SOUND of their
hammering echoes from the surrounding stone walls.

Note that because it is a working document, special requirements are capitalised. TWO MEN, for example will be needed, probably extras. If they were featured characters, their names would be capitalised. Attention is also directed to the sound effect the scene requires.

2. INT. CONDEMNED CELL. DAY

MARIA is young and beautiful; sensitive, fiery and emotional. As her face, in B.C.U., enters FRAME, we notice the fear in her eyes. Her mouth is trembling slightly while O.S. the awful pounding of the hammers continues. She closes her eyes against the SOUND, as if to try and cut it out.

Again, there are different schools of thought about the style of presentation. I belong to the old-fashioned one which believes that the object of the document is to demonstrate to the reader as exactly as possible what it is that the writer wants to see up on the screen. I am not trying to take the director's job and I know that he will shoot what he wants to shoot but this is *my* vision. Damn it all, I am the writer. Note the brief encapsulation of Maria's character. Names will always be in upper case. Some people think once the character is established, it is no longer necessary to capitalise the name in description. I do not.

B.C.U. means big close-up. FRAME is the picture area. O.S. is what is happening off-screen, as opposed to VOICE OVER (V.O.), for example, which is used for narrative or indicating thoughts. The use of camera directions is also controversial. I believe the device shows precisely the picture the author envisages. Certainly it could be written:

We see Maria in the condemned cell. She is young, beautiful, fiery and emotional. We also see the fear in her eyes. Outside, the pounding of the hammers continues. She closes her eyes against the sound.

She has got to be in FRAME for us to see her. We will not see the fear in her eyes without a C.U. at least. The SOUND will have to be heard O.S. if you are going to recreate the paragraph written above. So what is the problem for the director unless he wants to shoot something else altogether?

The fact of the matter is that what appears on the screen is what the CAMERA sees and so for me it is logical to describe what the camera does. This is not taking away from what the director will do or what the cinematographer will want to do: making pictures is a collaborative exercise; we all want the best from everyone. But the script is and always will be the starting point. I want the reader to see in imagination the same picture I visualise. If we are in production, that representation was obviously good enough for the producer to buy: all we want now is for the director to realise it. I do not know of any bad scripts that have become good films. I know of plenty of fine ones that have become lousy films.

I tend to use the camera like this:

110. INT. FARMHOUSE. NIGHT.

CAMERA PANS AWAY from a B.C.U. of a lighted candle to CLOSE-UP of GUTMAN as he sips at his soup.

He is dining with FERNANDEZ, CARLO and a good-looking young officer, RAPHAEL. GUTMAN raises his glass of wine to toast them all.

Between scenes there can be directions to FADE or DISSOLVE, which are placed bottom right of the scene, to denote a passage of time. However these days one mostly just CUTS, regardless, so there is no need to write CUT TO. Cutting from one scene to another, to pause briefly in time, I have used the device of the candle-flame. RAPHAEL is introduced for the first time and so merits a description.

With four people talking around the table, I have made no effort to elaborate on the camera action. There will obviously be a lot of inter-cutting from one to the other. This fine-detailing of scenes is plainly for the director to determine with his cinematographer, and may well involve the editor as well.

Dialogue is centred and at about two thirds of the width of the descriptive lines. Scenes continued over page will be marked OVER/ at the bottom and then marked CONT/ on the next page, together with a repetition of the scene number. Dialogue that is broken up will also be marked (CONT.). This is not fussiness. It helps to make clear that a speech has not been left out, since conversations are between two or more people. For example:-

110. CONT/

GUTMAN (CONT.)

There is only one item on the agenda. How to kill the President.

Mark the script firmly END. FADE OUT could be to another scene. Pages do go missing. Remember the title page. It is most important because it establishes your ownership. In the centre it will have the title of your work and below that your name: I like to use capitals.

Bottom right will be listed your name and address with telephone/ mobile/fax/e-mail numbers. This is the point of contact. If you are using an agency put *their* name and details – or they may just put a sticker over. Bottom left will be your name again after a copyright symbol and the year-date. If you have registered the script, with the Writers' Guild for example, you may want to make a note of that there too. It is important to register your ownership of the copyright of your screenplay. It may one day be of great value and you do not want anyone to try to filch it from you. Sammy Glick is still alive and well, and living in the Hollywood Hills, as well as working at the BBC.

A few more tips:

- Always submit screenplays that are printed on clean white paper, updated and fresh-looking. No one wants to consider a script that has been around.
- Make sure it is in the present tense. Film is immediate. Make sure it is in reasonably good English. Even the grammar of university graduates tends to be pretty slip-shod these days, as is their spelling. There is no excuse for the latter: the computer can do that (remember though, if you put in the *wrong* word, so long as it is spelled correctly, it will check out OK). As for the former, you are claiming to be a writer: you are supposed to be literate. If you are dyslexic, people will make allowances: it is the power of your imagination that counts.
- Do not make alterations or corrections in pen or pencil: again there is no excuse for not amending the script when you own a word-processor, God's great gift to writers.
- Some people, for reasons unknown to me, are fussy about spiral binders. I like them. They allow the script to be opened out flat and even folded back on itself. I cannot imagine anything more convenient for the reader.
- Remember there is no such thing as *the* screenplay until it becomes a shooting script. Until then it is the first, second, third draft and so on *ad infinitum*. You must work and re-work your screenplay until it meets your satisfaction. One day a producer will accept it and appoint a director and they will re-work it all over again. As Sam Spiegel might have said: 'That is life, baby.'
- The director will also not take notice of any parenthetical instructions attached to the dialogue, and nor most likely will the actors. I still defend their use from time to time. After all, it can be another way of spelling out the sub-text. I realise, unless I am Stephen King, that no one is interested in what I want but what the hell, I wrote it and that is how I see it.

A FINAL RECAP

The object of the script in the first place is to make someone read it. So long as it fulfils that purpose, it does not matter how it is set out but there is a standard form of presentation which has been outlined.

That fine writer John Milius, whose important screen credits include *Apocalypse Now* and *The Wind and the Lion*, advises that camera directions should be omitted altogether on the grounds that they are presumptuous. He believes the only admissible instructions are those indicating night or day but these are something of an anachronism with the new technologies available. It used to be important whether the crew was working during the day or at night, which was more difficult and much more expensive. Most lighting effects are now achieved electronically.

Milius also believes that a screenplay should read like a novel. I take it by this he means that it should be sharp and clear and interesting to read, which indeed it should, but there are major differences. A screenplay is always written in the present tense, as it happens up there on the screen: most novels would read awkwardly in that form. Novels might include pages of description about the background, the settings, which are necessary for us to form a clear image of the scene in our imagination. We do not imagine what is on-screen: it is there. Novels can freewheel at length about the innermost thoughts of their characters. We must establish those thoughts in some other way and in brief shots. The novel can – must – give exhaustive descriptions of its characters. We *show* who they are and what they do in the course of the exposition of our conflict. We are approaching them from quite different angles.

Novels have no temporal, spatial or geographic restrictions which means they are not bound by budgets. There are few, if any, directors in the world who get a blank cheque to make a film. Even David Lean had to make budgetary compromises. At the lower end of production, particularly on television, budgets become even more important, indeed there is a constant squeeze on them to maintain the competitiveness of the production company.

A professional writer, as you wish to be, will have to adopt a variety of skills according to the medium in which he is working. There is a whole range of programmes on television – and radio – which will require the input of a writer. The great bulk of film production in the UK is for training and corporate films, documentaries – not feature films. To write the scenario of a major movie is your goal: there are many paths to that end and you will have to be extremely flexible in the practice of your craft unless you want to be very poor. I sometimes claim I can write a script on a cash register, by which I mean that as I write I take in all the considerations of the budget. Screenplays determine budget – in the first place, anyway.

To return to style, what is all-important is to make your intentions clear. You will need to number your scenes for continuity but even without the instructions for INT/EXT or DAY/NIGHT it is obvious what is required for this shot – the first of Anthony Simmons' *The Optimists of Nine Elms*:

> 1. A vista of crowded emptiness, of narrow streets and smoke-stained railway cuttings. A huge gasworks dominates the skyline like a grim monument. We are witnessing the beginning of the end of one whole area of London.

When the Production Designer and the Assistant Directors, and others, begin the task of breaking the script down, they will know its requirements. Until that time, without any jargon, it evokes the picture on screen for the reader. That is all that matters.

MARKETING YOUR SCRIPT

The good news is that every producer out there is looking for the script that will make the movie that will bankroll him to moor a yacht in Cannes harbour. He does not even mind if it is by an unknown – it will cost him less – so long as it is a vehicle that will attract star names. With a bankable cast and director, he will be able to raise the money.

The bad news is a) that tens of thousands of other writers are competing with you and b) the odds against *your* script ever falling across the desk of *that* producer (i.e. the one who has faith in you) are stacked high.

For a start, he receives hundreds of scripts per week. He, and again I mean the person who actually makes decisions (these days more likely to be a she) cannot read them all and so has to delegate the task, generally to recently graduated *readers*, who have probably only taken this job as a stepping stone to getting *their* screenplay produced, so they will not have a lot of time for yours.

And since they are unsuccessful writers themselves, how is it likely that they will possess the analytical skills to judge yours? Indeed, if your script ever does reach the desk of that producer, does *he* – or *she* – have those skills? There are far, far more brilliant screenplays languishing away in bottom drawers than there are mediocre ones that have been made. The whole business is a big gamble. Do not be in any doubt about that.

Let us now take a look at some of the players around the roulette table.

THE PRODUCER

The title *producer* can mean many things. If the person who raised the money, or the studio executive who green-lighted the project, is prepared to accept the title *executive producer,* then it could be the person who actually oversees the production, though this is more frequently the *production supervisor* or *production manager.* Otherwise, and when the term is used in this book, *producer* means the person who made all the arrangements for the production, found the original material, funded the screenplay, hired the director and major stars, raised the money.

Not all producers are cigar-chewing movie moguls behind opulent desks. Some of them do not even have an office and operate on the move from a mobile phone – it used to be a telephone booth. Producers come in all shapes and sizes and their status is accorded on the strength of their credits and how much those films took at the box office. They are not all brash entrepreneurs. There are many who have taste and refinement, people like Saul Zaentz for example (*Amadeus*, *One Flew Over the Cuckoo's Nest*, and many other fine films).

They tend not to have a lot of faith in writers, hiring and firing them at will. They sometimes change directors as well. This tends not to happen so much in the UK, not out of innate decency but because the budget will not stand more than one director and one-and-a-half writers. This may be why the script is so often identified in the UK as being the industry's principal problem. Most tip-top films have had more than one writer employed on them, even though a single name shows on the credits. Money takes precedence above credit for the average writer. In the USA gangs of writers turn out brilliant sit-coms lasting little more than 20 minutes, like *Frasier*. In the UK a whole comedy series, maybe running for years, will use just one writer.

The best producers are perfectionists, as are the best directors, and will not go on the floor with their movie until all the ingredients are exactly right – a miracle of logistics in itself. Spiegel and Lean spent years developing their projects. Sometimes the writer is part of the team, as Robert Bolt was. The important thing to remember about the producer is that he *owns* the film. Under European law he shares the ownership of the copyright (as co-author) with the director of the film. But he makes the financial arrangements and will control the net producer's receipts. So it by no means follows that they are equal partners in the project.

THE DIRECTOR

There are some instances where the producer is the leading creative light in a production but the responsibility for the film is almost invariably accorded to the director. The producer makes sure the picture stays on budget and he will be responsible for delivering the end product to the distributor. Only a few directors in the world get what is known as the final cut. Even David Lean had to give way sometimes. A film may be a work of art but it was made as a commercial enterprise and those who invested their millions will want to see a good return.

Directors have big egos. They need them, for their job is a demanding one, controlling temperamental artistes, bolshie technicians and awkward writers who do not understand that their services are no longer required. That is not entirely true, of course. There are directors who will welcome the writer on set and ask his advice while filming, but not many. The director wants to see his work up on the screen and he will squeeze every last buck out of the budget, and more if he can, while the producer is there to encourage and threaten, and make sure he does not.

The director knows that his future career depends on how well his film turns out and how much it makes at the box office. If it is a smash hit, they will be queuing up for his talents. No one will remember how much it cost, just how much profit it made. So he will wring the very best out of all those working on the film; the writer, the cinematographer, the editor, the actors and all the technicians, of whom there are many. Making a film is a major logistical exercise and, although the producer is nominally in charge, once the camera turns it is the director who will be the major influence in the determination of whether that exercise is a success or not. It is in their nature to be exploitative. Some are monsters whom you will come to hate. But on the first night, all is forgotten.

THE CAST

Actors can be monsters too. They tend to be very introspective. It is a curious profession, pretending to be someone else, indeed trying to *be* someone else. It can be mentally destructive. The very top actors can be very pleasant and social, or monomaniacs who hide behind their entourages. The rest of the cast can be great fun to work with – after all, actors are entertainers.

Their physical appearance will almost certainly not be like that which you had envisaged for your characters. To begin with, the top names will have been engaged for their box-office value. It sounds crazy but those massive investments must be justified. You may know someone who is recognised as the best actor in England, playing at the National Theatre, say, but unless he or she has valuable screen credits, no one will want to know. Everyone likes to play safe.

That is why the source material is often a best-selling novel: it already has a market. The director and the actors have their own followers. Not many (script) writers do. But the big pulling factor in any film will always be the star. People go to see Clint Eastwood or Julia Roberts or Tom Cruise. The value of their names above the marquee can be actuarially predicted. The picture can still fail of course – ask a big star like Kevin Costner. But Mel Gibson's name attached to your screenplay is as safe as it gets – for now!

THE AGENT

Agents can be very powerful people. In Hollywood they often become producers or studio heads and run the show. They control the *talent* and the talent sells the picture. There are literary agents who deal with publishers and producers, and there are minor conglomerates that handle writers, directors, actors and even directors and producers. A good agent can make all the difference to your career.

Do not ask me who the top agents are. The question is irrelevant right now. You will be lucky to find *any* agent who will accept you. Agents have overheads and it costs them money to represent you. If you are not an earner it will be the other clients who subsidise you. Agents will charge you anything between ten and fifteen per cent of your earnings, even more if it comes from overseas. Percentages are negotiable but not for you if you are just starting.

How do you get an agent? Well, usually they find you. They know their business depends on the success of their clients and the constant infusion of new blood. So they go to the theatre, to fringe productions as well as mainstream ones, or to Film School shows. They read any reviews they can get their hands on. What they do not do is read unsolicited material. They know, if they did, they would be flooded with it. You could write or telephone and ask them if they would read your work: if you impress them, they might. Even then the chances are that your script will be read by some junior in the office, who might not choose to pass it on.

If you could write a play for lunchtime theatre, it would give you a chance to display your literary skills as it would if you wrote a short piece for students to film. You could try the corporate sector. That is where I did my first actual film work, making a sales film for Ford trucks. I also made some shorts for the cinema although, sadly, that is not a market any more – although they do commission some for television. The point is to have something to show.

Otherwise you will have to rely on recommendation, possibly through other clients of the agency. A multi-faceted agency that has a television name on their books, for example, one of the stars of a soap, will have a relationship with the producer and may be able to get you tried out on the writing team. What will never get you anywhere is stuffing scripts in a desk drawer. Keep working, at any level, so long as you are practising your craft.

Finally, remember an agency is not an employment agency and if you ring up every day to find out what work they have for you, you will not last long on their books. Of course they will seek to get you work but you will have to put yourself about as well. What agents are good at is vetting your contracts and collecting the money – and do not knock that, it is a valuable service. They will also seek to get introductions for you and then it is up to you to sell yourself. Your secret weapon is the script in your briefcase. If it is good enough, the words will sell it for you. No one will engage you on the strength of a pitch: in the last resort they always want words on paper. Just make sure your words are good enough.

UNIONS

From the moment your first script is accepted and you become a professional writer, you may break open the champagne but do not rejoice too much for your troubles are only just starting. Has anyone actually given you any money yet, or a contract? What does the contract say?

From the very beginning, you should of course take advice. Go to your agent, if you have one, and make sure that they thoroughly vet whatever proposal has been made. Be sure that the terms are satisfactory to you, personally. It is a great temptation, in order to earn a first credit, to work for nothing if asked. Try to avoid this. There is a great deal of speculative film-making, usually conducted on the basis of deferring fees. If you want to be a professional writer, this is no way to work. Many people fall for it, simply in order to earn a credit, but the bulk of these pictures are never even distributed – so what is the point of a credit that no one will ever see?

Even legitimate film-makers will try to cut corners to pay less than the going rates. And many of them run out of money in the course of the production, which means you may have problems in getting paid. Again, a massive payment on the first day of shooting is of no use to anyone if that first day never comes. To assist you with difficulties like these, it would be wise for you to join a union.

BECTU (Broadcasting, Entertainment, Cinema and Theatre Union) has about 25,000 members in the fields encompassed by its name. It has a writers' section but will be of principal interest to those scenarists who have additional ambitions, such as being a director. Active membership is encouraged and you will have the opportunity to meet other workers in the industry. The union represents directors, producers, cameramen and technicians generally, both in film and television. It has an open door policy regarding membership, with a good record of successful legal action on behalf of its members, and there is a graduates' branch as well. A list of benefits, the BECTU100, is available from the address below. Specialist consultants are available for members who need advice concerning tax, copyright, or contracts. It has agreements with PACT (Producers' Alliance for Cinema and Television) and most of the broadcasters, but the only writing agreement it has is for short films and documentaries. It will, however, back any of its writers' claims based on the agreements of the WGGB (Writers' Guild of Great Britain). Enquiries may be made to:

The General Secretary
BECTU
111 Wardour Street
London
W1V 4AY
telephone: 0207 437 8056
website: www.bectu.org.uk

The WGGB does have agreements for writers with all the major broad-casters and with PACT. The latter is currently being re-negotiated following successful action against employers by the Writers' Guilds of America, both East and West. An important benefit for screenwriters belonging to the WGGB is that in the event of their working in the United States, where membership of the Writers' Guild is obligatory and costs $2,500, they do not have to pay the joining fee. The Guild also has Minimum Terms Agreements with many major publishers, theatre and radio employers. There is a pension scheme for radio and television writers. There are two grades of membership, 'Candidate' (for would-be professionals) and 'Full' (for those with writing credits). Active membership is encouraged and the Guild holds a number of events throughout the year where you can meet with other writers. Chief among these is the Annual Awards Ceremony. Other Guild benefits are automatic membership of ALCS (the Authors' Licensing & Collecting Society) and free access to the British Library reading rooms for research. There is a Guild Bulletin which is published ten times a year. The Guild is a recognised Trade Union but without any party political affiliation. Enquiries can be made to:

The General Secretary
WGGB
430 Edgware Road
London
W2 1EH
telephone: 0207 723 8074
website: www.writers.org.uk/guild

THE FILM COUNCIL

There used to be a number of disparate organisations intended to assist film-makers, like *British Screen,* the *British Film Institute* production fund, the *British Film Commission* and the Arts Council of England's *Lottery Film Department.* Now, fortunately, they are all gathered under one umbrella, that of the Film Council. I say 'fortunately' but this is speculative since it only got underway in 2001, although it had been planned for some time, and we will have to wait and see what results it produces.

When the Government created the Film Council, it was warmly welcomed by most bodies within the industry, many of which were disenchanted with the way its funding had been apparently thrown down the drain by the *Lotteries Film Department* and the string of appalling flops it backed with our money. Now, at last, we were to have a lead body for film in the United Kingdom which can provide strategic leadership for the whole film sector. It can encourage greater effectiveness and efficiency and address not only cultural development but also the market failures which so depressingly characterised British film. Its remit covers the development of all film, television and moving image technologies.

The Film Council is committed to training and developing new talent. It is acutely aware that moving image education in the UK has developed in a random and piecemeal fashion over the last half century and intends to provide cohesive infrastructural support in this field through a strategy which will bring together a range of different organisations. These include cinemas, educational institutions, libraries, archives, film societies, and production and training centres.

It will take time for the Film Council to have an impact on the industry but I believe its initiation was a well-thought out, logical step. I believe it will make a marked difference and I am encouraged by talks I have had with Alan Parker (Chairman) – at last, a famous British film-maker in charge – and John Woodward (Director) that they mean to do what they say. Both see the role of screen-writing as being at the very heart of good film-making and essential to a reformation of the industry. To this end, they are allocating substantial funds for assistance in this field, determined to offer every possible encouragement to screenwriters, to develop their skills.

Working with *Skillset*, the National Training Organisation for film, *The Film Council* is providing support through its training fund for various initiatives which include:

- Introductory courses across the UK for aspiring screenwriters.
- Intensive full- and part-time courses for screenwriters with limited experience.
- A service providing readers for screenplays.
- A series of regular workshops for screenwriters.
- A rehearsed reading service, giving the opportunity for draft scripts to be dramatised in front of an audience.

Enquiries should be made to:

The Film Council
10 Little Portland Street
LONDON
W1W 7JG
telephone: 0207 861 7861
website: www.filmcouncil.org.uk

TRAINING

Training is obviously helpful if you can get it and if you can afford it. Take advantage of any of the schemes offered by the Film Council, if you can. Beware of cowboys: there are a lot of them out there. So many people want to get into this business that training has become a growth sector. You can depend on any courses recommended by Skillset because they are all thoroughly vetted, but they do cost.

Skillset is working closely with the Film Council on its strategy to provide training to screenwriters. In particular, they will be working together to create an accreditation system for script-writing courses currently provided by Higher Education institutions. The object of this is to ensure that courses have proper links with the film industry and provide the most appropriate training needed for students to find work once they have left.

There are other perfectly legitimate bodies like the Screenwriters' Workshop which offers a script assessment service as well as courses in general screenwriting, documentary, comedy and script editing (for those with credits). They also have events and panel discussions, as do Peeping Toms (for film-makers generally) and Women in Film, whose work is self-explanatory. These organisations are all good for networking, at not too exorbitant a cost.

The quality of training depends of course upon the trainer. Script-writing is not easily taught by correspondence courses or even in classes, since every script is essentially an individual exercise. I have spent many hours with writers, going over just one screenplay, though I hope what the writer learned went way beyond the merits or demerits of that particular script.

The Screenwriters' Workshop
Suffolk House
1-8 Whitfield Place
London
W1P 5SF
telephone: 0207 387 5511
website: www.lsw.org.uk

Skillset
103 Dean Street
London
W1V 5AR
telephone: 0207 534 5302

Any professional advice you can get is useful but you can do it alone. If you can absorb all the principles stated in this book and learn to apply them to your work, you *will* be able to turn out screenplays that are both workable and acceptable.

I wish you well. Let me know when you are famous.

FILMOGRAPHY

* denotes films highly recommended for viewing

2001: A Space Odyssey (1968) – dir. Stanley Kubrick, writ. Arthur C.
Clarke, Stanley Kubrick

Absolute Beginners (1986) – dir. Julien Temple, writ. Richard Burridge,
Tom MacPherson

The Adventures of Tom Jones (1963) – dir. Tony Richardson, writ. Jeremy
Lloyd from the novel by Henry Fielding.

African Queen, The (1951) – dir. John Huston, writ. James Agee from the
novel by C. S. Forester

* *Alfie* (1965) – dir. Lewis Gilbert, writ. Bill Naughton from his play

Alien (1979) – dir. Ridley Scott, writ. Dan O'Bannon, Ronald Shusett

* *All Quiet on the Western Front* (1930) – dir. Lewis Milestone, writ. George
Abbott, Del Andrews, Maxwell Anderson from the novel by Erich Maria
Remarque

Amadeus (1984) – dir. Milos Forman, writ. Peter Schaffer from his play

* *American Beauty* (1999) – dir. Sam Mendes, writ. Alan Ball

Anzio (1968) – dir. Edward Dmytryk, writ. A. L. Craig, Frank de Felitta

Apocalypse Now (1979) – dir. Francis Ford Coppola, writ. John Milius from
the novel *Heart of Darkness* by Joseph Conrad

* *As Good As It Gets* (1997) – dir. James L. Brooks, writ. Mark Andras,
James L. Brooks

Barbarella (1968) – dir. Roger Vadim, writ. Terry Southern, Roger Vadim,

Tudor Gates, et al.

* *Battleship Potemkin, The* (1925) – dir. Sergei Eisenstein, writ. Nina Agadzhanova, Sergei Eisenstein

Better a Widow (1969) – dir. Duccio Tessari, writ. Tudor Gates

* *Bicycle Thieves* (1948) – dir. Vittorio de Sica, writ. Vittorio de Sica, Cesare Zavatini, Suso Cecchi D'Amico, Oreste Biancoli, Adolfo Frani, Gherardo Gherardi, Garado Guerrieri, from the novel by Luigi Bartolini

* *Big Sleep, The* (1946) – dir. Howard Hawkes, writ. William Faulkner from the novel by Raymond Chandler

Bonfire of the Vanities (1999) – dir. Brian de Palma, writ. Michael Christopher from the novel by Tom Wolfe

* *Bridge on the River Kwai* (1957) – dir. David Lean, writ. Carl Foreman, Michael Wilson, Pierre Boulle from his novel

Bridges of Madison County, The (1995) – dir. Clint Eastwood, writ. Roger James Waller from his novel, Richard la Gravenese

Cabaret (1972) – dir. Bob Fosse, writ. Jay Presson from the play by John van Druten, based on Christopher Isherwood's Berlin Stories

Carrie (1976) – dir. Brian de Palma, writ. Lawrence D. Cohen from the novel by Stephen King

Casablanca (1942) – dir. Michael Curtiz, writ. Murray Burnett, Julius J. Epstein, Philip G. Eptein, Howard Coch from Joan Alison's play

Chariots of Fire (1981) – dir. Hugh Hudson, writ. Colin Welland

* *City Lights* (1931) – dir. and writ. Charlie Chaplin

CutThroat Island (1995) – dir. Renny Harlin, writ. Michael Frost Bestner, James Gorman

Cyrano de Bergerac – (1950) dir. Michael Gordon, writ. Carl Foreman

Cyrano de Bergerac – (1990) dir. Jean-Paul Rappeneau, writ. Jean-Paul Carrière

Danger Diabolik (1968) – dir. Mario Bava, writ. Tudor Gates, Brian Degas

Darling (1965) – dir. John Schlesinger, writ. Frederick Raphael

Dateline Diamonds (1966) – dir. Jeremy Summers, writ. Tudor Gates

Bridget Jones's Diary (2001) – dir. Sharon Maguire, writ. Helen Fielding from her novel, Andrew Davies, Richard Curtis

Dirty Rotten Scoundrels (1988) – dir. Frank Oz, writ. Dale Launer, Stanley Shapiro, Paul Hennings

* *Double Indemnity* (1944) – dir. Billy Wilder, writ. Billy Wilder and Raymond Chandler from the novel by James N. Cain

Dr Zhivago (1965) – dir. David Lean, writ. Robert Bolt based on the novel by Boris Pasternak

* *Duck Soup* (1933) – dir. Leo McCarey, writ. Bert Kalmar, Harry Ruby

E.T. (1982) – dir. Steven Spielberg, writ. Melissa Mathison

English Patient, The (1996) – dir. and writ. Anthony Minghella from the novel by Michael Ondaatje

* *Erin Brockovich* (2000) – dir. Steven Soderbergh, writ. Susannah Grant

Forrest Gump (1994) – dir. Robert Zemeckis, Eric Roth from the novel by Winton Groom

Forty-Ninth Parallel, The (1941) – dir. Michael Powell, writ. Rodney Ackland, Emerick Pressburger

Four in the Morning (1966) – dir. and writ. Anthony Simmons

Four Weddings and a Funeral (1994) – dir. Mike Newell, writ. Richard Curtis

French Connection, The (1971) – dir. William Friedkin, writ. Ernest Tidyman from the novel by Robin Moore

Friday the 13th (1980) – dir. Sean S. Cunningham, writ. Sean S. Cunningham, Victor Miller

Full Metal Jacket (1987) – dir. Stanley Kubrick, writ. Gustav Hasford, Michael Herr, Stanley Kubrick

Full Monty, The (1997) – dir. Peter Cattaneo, writ. Simon Beaufoy

Gandhi (1982) – dir. Richard Attenborough, writ. John Briley

General, The (1926) – dir. Buster Keaton, writ. Buster Keaton, Al Boasberg from the novel by William Pittenberger

Gladiator (2000) – dir. Ridley Scott, writ. David H. Razoni, John Logan, William Nicholson

Godfather, The (1972) – dir. Francis Ford Coppola, writ. Francis Ford Coppola and Mario Puzo from his novel

* *Gold Rush, The* (1925) – dir. and writ. Charlie Chaplin

GoldenEye (1995) – dir. Martin Campbell, writ. Michael France, Jeffrey Caine, Bruce Feirstein

Gone With The Wind (1939) – dir. Victor Fleming, writ. Sidney Howard from the novel by Margaret Mitchell

Great Train Robbery (1903) – dir. and writ. Edwin Porter

* *Gregory's Girl* (1980) – dir. and writ. Bill Forsyth

Halloween (1978) – dir. John Carpenter, writ. John Carpenter, Debra Hill

Hamlet (1969) – dir. and writ. Tony Richardson

Harry, He Is Here to Help (2000) – dir. Dominik Moll, writ. Dominik Moll, Gilles Marchand

Hatful of Rain, A (1957) – dir. Fred Zinnemann, writ. Michael V. Gazzo from his play

Heaven's Gate (1980) – dir. and writ. Michael Cimino

Henry V (1949) – dir. Laurence Olivier, Reginald Beck, writ. Lawrence Olivier, Alan Dent, Dallas Bower

In Which We Serve (1942) – dir. Noël Coward, writ. Noël Coward, David Lean

Indiana Jones and the Temple of Doom (1984) – dir. Steven Spielberg, writ. George Lucas, Willard Huyck, Gloria Katz

Ipcress File, The (1965) – dir. Sidney J. Furie, writ. Bill Canaway, James Doran from the novel by Len Deighton

Ishtar (1987) – dir. and writ. Elaine May

* *It's a Wonderful Life* (1946) – dir. Frank Capra, writ. Francis Goodrich, Albert Hackett, Frank Capra from Philip van Doren Stern's story

Jaws (1975) – dir. Steven Spielberg, writ. Carl Gottlieb and Peter Benchley from his novel

Jazz Singer, The (1927) – dir. Alan Crosland, writ. Alfred A. Cohen

Julius Caesar – (1955) dir. and writ. Joseph L. Mankiewicz

Kes (1969) – dir. Ken Loach, writ. Tony Garnett, Ken Loach from the novel by Barry Hines

Lawrence of Arabia (1962) – dir. David Lean, writ. Robert Bolt, Michael Wilson from *The Seven Pillars of Wisdon* by T. E. Lawrence

Lost Weekend, The (1945) – dir. Billy Wilder, writ. Billy Wilder, Charles Brackett from the novel by Charles R. Jackson

Love Story (1970) – dir. Arthur Hiller, writ. Erich Segal from his novel

Lust for a Vampire (1971) – dir. Jimmy Sangster, writ. Tudor Gates based on a story by Sheridan le Fanu

M*A*S*H. (1970) – dir. Robert Altman, writ. Richard Hooker from the novel by Ring Lardner

* *Maltese Falcon, The* (1941) – dir. and writ. John Huston from the novel by Dashiel Hammett

Mask of Zorro, The (1998) – dir. Martin Campbell, writ. John Eskow, Ted Elliott, Terry Rossio

Nashville (1975) – dir. Robert Altman, writ. John Tewkesbury

Night at the Opera, A (1935) – dir. Sam Wood, writ. James K. McGuinness, George Kaufman, Morrie Ryskind

Nightmare on Elm Street, A (1984) – dir. and writ. Wes Craven

Omen, The (1976) – dir. Richard Donner, writ. David Seltzer

On the Waterfront (1954) – dir. Elia Kazan, writ. Budd Schulberg

* *Once Upon a Time in America* (1984) – dir. Sergio Leone, writ. Leonardo Benvenuti, Piero De Bernardi, Enrico Medioli, Franco Arcalli, Franco Ferrini, Sergio Leone

One Flew Over the Cuckoo's Nest (1975) – dir. Milos Forman, writ. Bo Goldman, Lawrence Hauben from the novel by Ken Kessey

The Optimists of Nine Elms, The (1973) – dir. Anthony Simmons, writ. Tudor Gates, Anthony Simmons from his novel

Phantom of the Opera, The (1925) – dir. Rupert Julian, writ. Elliot J. Clawson

Pimpernel Smith (1942) – dir. Ian Dalrymple, writ. Anatole de Grunwald, A. G. MacDonald, Roland Pertwee

Play It Again, Sam (1972) – dir. and writ. Woody Allen from his play

Postman, The (1997) – dir. Kevin Costner, writ. Erich Roch, Brian Hedgeland

Prince of Tides (1991) – dir. Barbra Streisand, writ. Pat Conroy, Becky Johnston

* *Psycho* (1960) – dir. Alfred Hitchcock, writ. Joseph Stefano from the novel by Robert Bloch

* *Pulp Fiction* (1994) – dir. Quentin Tarantino, writ. Quentin Tarantino, John Avary

* *Raging Bull* (1980) – dir. Martin Scorcese, writ John Carpenter

* *Rashomon* (1950) – dir. Akira Kurosawa, writ Akira Kurosawa, Shirobu Hashimoto

Reflections in a Golden Eye (1967) – dir. John Huston, writ. Gladys Hill, Chapman Mortimer

* *Reservoir Dogs* (1992) – dir. Quentin Tarantino, writ. Quentin Tarantino, John Avary

Revolution (1985) – dir. Hugh Hudson, writ. Robert Dillon

01 THE HORROR GENRE
FROM BEELZEBUB TO BLAIR WITCH

Paul Wells   ISBN 1-903364-00-0   144pp

The inaugral book in the *Short Cuts* series is a comprehensive introduction to the history and key themes of the horror genre. The main issues and debates raised by horror, and the approaches and theories that have been applied to horror texts are all addressed. In charting the evolution of the horror film in social and cultural context, Paul Wells explores how it has reflected and commented upon particular historical periods, and asks how it may respond to the new millennium by citing recent innovations in the genre's development, such as the 'urban myth' narrative underpinning *Candyman* and *The Blair Witch Project*.

"An informed and highly readable account that is theoretically broad, benefiting from a wide range of cinematic examples."

Xavier Mendik, University College Northampton

02 THE STAR SYSTEM
HOLLYWOOD'S PRODUCTION OF POPULAR IDENTITIES

Paul McDonald   ISBN 1-903364-02-7   144pp

The Star System looks at the development and changing organization of the star system in the American film industry. Tracing the popularity of star performers from the early 'cinema of attractions' to the internet universe, Paul McDonald explores the ways in which Hollywood has made and sold its stars. Through focusing on particular historical periods, the key conditions influencing the star system in silent cinema, the studioera and the New Hollywood are discussed and illustrated by cases studies of Mary Pickford, Bette Davis, James Cagney, Julia Roberts, Tom Cruise, and Will Smith.

"A very good introduction to the topic filling an existing gap in the needs of researchers and students of the subject."

Roberta Pearson, University of Wales, Cardiff

03 SCIENCE FICTION CINEMA
FROM OUTERSPACE TO CYBERSPACE

Geoff King and Tanya Krzywinska   ISBN 1-903364-03-5   144pp

Science Fiction Cinema charts the dimensions of one of the most popular film genres. From lurid comic-book blockbusters to dark dystopian visions, science fiction is seen as both a powerful cultural barometer of our times and the product of particular industrial and commercial frameworks. The authors outline the major themes of the genre, from representations of the mad scientist and computer hacker to the relationship between science fiction and postmodernism, exploring issues such as the meaning of special effects and the influence of science fiction cinema on the entertainment media of the digital age.

"The best overview of English-language science-fiction cinema published to date... thorough, clearly written and full of excellent examples. Highly recommended."

Steve Neale, Sheffield Hallam University

04   EARLY SOVIET CINEMA
INNOVATION. IDEOLOGY AND PROPAGANDA.

David Gillespie   ISBN 1-903364-04-3   144pp

Early Soviet Cinema examines the aesthetics of Soviet cinema during its 'golden age' of the 1920s, against a background of cultural ferment and the construction of a new socialist society. Separate chapters are devoted to the work of Sergei Eisenstein, Lev Kuleshov, Vsevolod Pudovkin, Dziga Vertov and Alexander Dovzhenko. Other major directors are also discussed at length. David Gillespie places primary focus on the text, with analysis concentrating on the artistic qualities, rather than the political implications, of each film. The result is not only a discussion of each director's contribution to the 'golden age' and to world cinema, but also an exploration of their own distinctive poetics.

"An excellent book ... Lively and informative, it fills a significant gap and deserves to be on reading lists wherever courses on Soviet cinema are run."

Graham Roberts, University of Surrey

05   READING HOLLYWOOD
SPACES AND MEANINGS IN AMERICAN FILM

Deborah Thomas   ISBN 1-903364-01-9   144pp

Reading Hollywood examines the treatment of space and narrative in a selection of classic films including *My Darling Clementine*, Its a *Wonderful Life* and *Vertigo*. Deborah Thomas employs a variety of arguments in exploring the reading of space and its meaning in Hollywood cinema, and film generally. Topics covered include the importance of space in defining genre (such as the necessity of an urban landscape for a gangster film to be a gangster film); the ambiguity of offscreen space and spectatorship (how an audience reads an unseen but inferred setting) and the use of spatially disruptive cinematic techniques such as flashback to construct meaning.

"Amongst the finest introductions to Hollywood in particular and Film Studies in general ... subtler, more complex, yet more readable than most of its rivals, many of which it will displace."

Professor Robin Wood, *CineAction!*

06   DISASTER MOVIES
THE CINEMA OF CATASTROPHE

Stephen Keane   ISBN 1-903364-05-1   144pp

Disaster Movies provides a comprehensive introduction to the history and development of the disaster genre. The 1950s sci-fi B-movies to high concept 1990s 'millennial movies', Stephen Keane looks at the ways in which the representation of disaster and its aftermath are borne out of both contextual considerations and the increasing commercial demands of contemporary Hollywood. Through detailed analyses of such films as *Airport*, *The Poseidon Adventure*, *Independence Day* and *Titanic*, the book explores the continual reworking of this, to-date, undervalued genre.

"Providing detailed consideration of key movies within their social and cultural context, this concise introduction serves its purpose well and should prove a useful teaching tool."

Nick Roddick

07 THE WESTERN GENRE
FROM LORDSBURG TO BIG WHISKEY

John Saunders   ISBN 1-903364-12-4   144pp

The Western Genre offers close readings of the definitive American film movement as represented by such leading exponents as John Ford, Howard Hawks and Sam Peckinpah. In his consideration of such iconic motifs as the Outlaw Hero and the Lone Rider, John Saunders traces the development of perennial aspects of the genre, its continuity and, importantly, its change. Representations of morality and masculinity are also foregrounded in consideration of the genres major stars John Wayne and Clint Eastwood, and the book includes a number of detailed analyses of such landmark films as Shane, Rio Bravo, The Wild Bunch and Unforgiven.

"A clear exposition of the major thematic currents of the genre providing attentive and illuminating reading of major examples."

Ed Buscombe, Editor of the BFI Companion to the Werstern

08 PSYCHOANALYSIS AND CINEMA
THE PLAY OF SHADOWS

Vicky Lebeau   ISNB 1-903364-19-1   144pp

The book examines the long and uneven history of developments in modern art, science and technology that brought pychoanalysis and the cinema together towards the end of the nineteenth century. Vicky Lebeau explores the subsequent encounters between the two: the seductions of psychoanalysis and cinema as converging, though distinct, ways of talking about dream and desire, image and illusion, shock and sexuality. Beginning with Freud's encounter with the spectacle of hysteria on display in fin-de-siècle Paris, this study offers a detailed reading of the texts and concepts which generated the field of psychoanalytic film theory.

"A very lucid and subtle exploration of the reception of Freud's theories and their relation to psychoanalysis's contemporary developments - cinema and modernism. One of the best introduction to psychoanalytic film theory available."

Elizabeth Cowie, University of Kent

09 COSTUME AND CINEMA
DRESS CODES IN POPULAR FILM

Sarah Street   1-903364-18-3   144pp

Costume and Cinema presents an overview of the literature on film costume, together with a series of detailed case studies which highlight how costume is a key signifier in film texts. Sarah Street demonstrates how costume relates in fundamental ways to the study of film narrative and mise-en-scène, in some cases constituting a language of its own. In particular the book foregrounds the related issues of adaptation and embodiment in a variety of different genres and films including Desperately Seeking Susan, Titanic and The Matrix.

"A valuable addition to the growing literature on film and costume ... engagingly written, offering a lucid introduction to the field."

Stella Bruzzi, Royal Holloway, University of London

10 MISE-EN-SCÈNE
Film Style and Interpretation

Iohn Gibbs   1-903364-06-X   144pp

Mise-en-scène explores and elucidates constructions of this fundamental concept in thinking about film. In uncovering the history of mise-en-scène within film criticism, and through the detailed exploration of scenes from films such as *Imitation of Life* and *Lone Star*, John Gibbs makes the case for the importance of a sensitive understanding of film style, and provides an introduction to the skills of close reading. This book thus celebrates film-making and film criticism alive to the creative possibilities of visual style.

"An immensely readable and sophisticated account of a topic of central importance to the serious study of films."

Deborah Thomas, University of Sunderland

11 NEW CHINESE CINEMA
CHALLENGING REPRESENTATIONS

Sheila Cornelius with Ian Haydn Smith   1-903364-13-2   144pp

New Chinese Cinema examines the 'search for roots' films that emerged from China in the aftermath of the Cultural Revolution. The authors contextualise the films of the so-called Fifth Generation directors who came to prominence in the 1980s and 1990s such as Chen Kaige, Zhang Yimou and Tian Zhuangzhuang. Including close analysis of such pivotal films as *Farewell My Concubine, Raise the Red Lantern* and *The Blue Kite*, the book also examines the rise of contemporary Sixth Generation underground directors whose themes embrace the disaffection of urban youth.

"Very thorough in its coverage of the historical and cultural background to New Chinese Cinema ... clearly written and appropriately targeted at an undergraduate audience."

Leon Hunt, Brunel University

13 ANIMATION
GENRE AND AUTHORSHIP

Paul Wells   1-903364-20-5   144pp

New Chinese Cinema examines the 'search for roots' films that emerged from China in the aftermath of the Cultural Revolution. The authors contextualise the films of the so-called Fifth Generation directors who came to prominence in the 1980s and 1990s such as Chen Kaige, Zhang Yimou and Tian Zhuangzhuang. Including close analysis of such pivotal films as *Farewell My Concubine, Raise the Red Lantern* and *The Blue Kite*, the book also examines the rise of contemporary Sixth Generation underground directors whose themes embrace the disaffection of urban youth.